Current Perspectives on Pronunciation:
Practices Anchored in Theory

Current Perspectives on Pronunciation: Practices Anchored in Theory

Joan Morley
Editor

Teachers of English to Speakers of Other Languages

Staff Editor: Julia Frank-McNeil
Editorial Assistant: Christopher R. Byrne

Copyright ©1987 by
Teachers of English to Speakers of Other Languages
Washington, D.C.
Printed in the U.S.A.

Library of Congress Catalog No. 86-051035
ISBN 0-939791-28-5

Preface

Beginning in the late 1960's and continuing into the 1970's and early 1980's, there was a significant decrease in the amount of time and explicit attention devoted to pronunciation teaching in English programs for second and foreign language learners. While publications of textbooks in a wide variety of other ESL/EFL areas mushroomed, very few new pronunciation books appeared on the market, and those most widely circulated can be counted on the fingers of one hand: J. Donald Bowen's *Patterns of English Pronunciation,* (1975), Newbury House, Rowley, Massachusetts; Joan Morley's *Improving Spoken English,* (1979), The University of Michigan Press, Ann Arbor; Judy B. Gilbert's *Clear Speech,* (1984), Cambridge University Press, New York; Clifford H. Prator and Betty Wallace Robinett's (4th edition) *Manual of American English Pronunciation,* (1985), Holt, Rinehart and Winston, New York.

Growing dissatisfaction with both the principles and the practices of the traditional approaches to pronunciation teaching led to the elimination of pronunciation work in many programs. Factors involved included changing models of second language learning, changing focus in second language teaching, and changing models of linguistic description. As directions in pedagogy moved to a concentration on language functions, communicative competencies, task-based methodologies, and realism and authenticity in learning activities and materials, the familiar ways and means of teaching pronunciation did not seem to fit in. In the eyes of both students and teachers, they lacked process appeal and product delivery.

Then, in the early 1980's there was a small groundswell of renewed interest in the learning/teaching of pronunciation, but with a redefinition of pronunciation so that it took on quite a new look. By the mid-1980's the modest groundswell had grown into a clear and definite trend toward a renewal of concern for and excitement about the pronunciation component of oral communication in second language theory and pedagogy.

Gradually, increasing numbers of programs have emerged that reflect a "new look" in pronunciation teaching. The very specific and very urgent needs of several special groups of ESL/EFL learners has been one of the major forces behind these new programs. The following groups of adult and teenage learners have challenged our ESL/EFL expertise as facilitators in the learning of pronunciation:

1. Foreign student teaching assistants in colleges and universities,

2. A growing population of foreign-born technical, business, and professional employees in business and industry,

3. Adult and teenage refugees in resettlement and vocational training programs,

4. International businessmen and businesswomen who need to use English as an international *lingua franca.*

A number of us, who believe that intelligible pronunciation is an essential component of communicative competence, have turned our attention to reassessing learner needs and learner goals, instructional objectives, and learning/teaching methodologies. Much of our work has been set within the wider framework of current directions in language learning, and teaching theory and pedagogy. One primary concern is how pronunciation fits into communicative language teaching.

The seven papers in this volume represent the work of eight language teachers, researchers and linguists who have a special interest in the pronunciation component of oral language: how it operates to transmit meaning, how it can be learned, and how teachers and teaching can facilitate learning. These papers were presented in a one-day colloquium held during the 19th Annual TESOL Convention in New York City, March 8, 1985. The title of the colloquium was "Current Perspectives on Pronunciation: Practices Anchored in Theory."

Both speakers and members of the audience during the colloquium noted the following themes which emerged across the balance of the presentations.

1. A focus on working with pronunciation as an integral part of, not apart from, oral communication.

2. A focus on the primary importance of suprasegmentals (i.e., stress, rhythm, intonation, etc.) and how they are used to communicate meaning, with a secondary importance assigned to segmentals (i.e., vowel and consonant sounds).

3. A special focus on syllable structure, linking (both within words and across word boundaries), phrase-group divisions (thought group chunking and pausing), phrasal stress and rhythm patterns.

4. Learner involvement in the learning/teaching process

including speech awareness and self-monitoring.

5. Meaningful practice set in speech activities suited to the communication styles in the learners' real-life situations.

6. A focus on providing speech modeling that is natural and contextual, and avoiding hypercorrect or "foreigner-talk" modeling.

In addition, it was also clear that two themes emerged that impact on teacher preparation programs for ESL/EFL careers.

1. A need to prepare teachers with a solid background in English phonetics and phonology, and its application to second and foreign language learning/teaching.

2. A need to prepare teachers with solid methodologies for teaching pronunciation as a part of communicative language teaching.

I believe it is not out of line to report that both presenters and audience members enjoyed and profited from this TESOL 1985 Colloquium. I am pleased to present the papers here for professional colleagues. The papers contain discussions that encompass a variety of aspects of the broad topic "Current Perspectives on Pronunciation," but overall they reflect the authors' enthusiasm, creative thinking, and yes, a sense of dedication to their very focused work.

Joan Morley
The University of Michigan

Contributors
(in alphabetical order)

Sandra C. Browne, Language Consultant; Educational Division, General Motors Research Laboratories, Warren, Michigan.

John C. Catford, Professor of Linguistics; former Chair, Department of Linguistics; former Director, English Language Institute, The University of Michigan.

Marianne Celce-Murcia, Associate Professor; ESL section, Department of English, The University of California at Los Angeles.

William W. Crawford, Adjunct Instructor; Division of English as a Foreign Language, Georgetown University.

Judy B. Gilbert, Language Consultant and author. (Former ESL Instructor, Hayward State University.)

Thomas N. Huckin, Associate Professor; Department of English, Carnegie-Mellon University.

Joan Morley, Associate Professor; Linguistics, English Language Institute, The University of Michigan.

Mary S. Temperley, visiting Assistant Professor; Division of English as a Second Language, University of Illinois at Urbana-Champaign; ESL Instructor, Urbana Adult Education Program.

Rita Wong, Assistant Director; American Language Institute, San Francisco State University.

Contents

1. Teaching Pronunciation as Communication
   Marianne Celce-Murcia   1

2. Learner Variables and Prepronunciation Considerations
   in Teaching Pronunciation
   Rita Wong   13

3. Pronunciation and Listening Comprehension
   Judy B. Gilbert   29

4. Pronunciation Tutorials for Nonnative Technical
   Professionals: A Program Description
   Sandra C. Browne and Thomas N. Huckin   41

5. Linking and Deletion in Final Consonant Clusters
   Mary S. Temperley   59

6. Phonetics and the Teaching of Pronunciation
   John C. Catford   83

7. The Pronunciation Monitor: L2 Acquisition
   Considerations and Pedagogical Priorities
   William W. Crawford   101

Editorial notes precede each paper in the collection.

Teaching Pronunciation as Communication

Marianne Celce-Murcia

The University of California at Los Angeles

Editorial Notes

In "Teaching Pronunciation as Communication" Marianne Celce-Murcia observes that whereas communicative techniques have become widely used in ESL teaching in general over the past 10 years, they have not been employed very much in the area of pronunciation instruction. She reviews conventional pronunciation teaching techniques briefly, pointing out their limitations; then she argues that pronunciation can be taught much more effectively in a way that is compatible with the communicative approach.

She goes on to suggest that pronunciation points can be taught communicatively — just as readily as grammar points, functions, and vocabulary items can be taught communicatively by presenting language through tasks that focus on meaningful interactions between and among students in role-playing, problem-solving, and game activities. She asserts that the same activities used to teach other language areas communicatively can be used to teach pronunciation communicatively. She then presents a very useful sampling of communicative activities that can be used in communicative pronunciation teaching.

In the final part of her paper Celce-Murcia outlines four steps for teachers who wish to develop their own programs.

1. Identify your students' problem areas.

2. Find lexical/grammatical contexts that have a number of natural occurrences of the problem sound(s).

3. Develop communicative tasks that incorporate the words.

4. Develop at least three or four exercises so that you can recycle the problem and keep providing students with practice of the target sound(s) but in new contexts.

J.M.

Teaching Pronunciation as Communication

The history of foreign language instruction reveals that there have been many differences of opinion over the years about the value of teaching pronunciation and about how best to teach it.[1] The *grammar-translation* and *reading-based approaches* have viewed pronunciation as irrelevant. The *direct method* has claimed that pronunciation is very important and presents it via teacher modeling; the teacher is ideally a native or near-native speaker of the target language. In the *audio-lingual approach* pronunciation is likewise very important. The teacher also models, and the students repeat; however, the teacher now has the assistance of a structurally-based teaching device: the minimal pair drill:[2]

    hit/heat
    rice/lice
    sin/sing

The *cognitive code approach* de-emphasized pronunciation in favor of grammar and vocabulary because the conventional wisdom of the late 1960's and early 1970's (see Scovel, 1969) held that native-like pronunciation could not be taught anyway. And, by extension, it was argued by many that pronunciation should not be taught at all.

More recently, however, the *communicative approach* has brought new urgency to the teaching of pronunciation, since it has been empirically demonstrated by Hinofotis and Bailey (1980) that there is a threshold level of pronunciation in English such that if a given non-native speaker's pronunciation falls below this level, he or she will not be able to communicate orally no matter how good his or her control of English grammar and vocabulary might be.[3] The problem teachers face is that there are currently no materials available for teaching pronunciation communicatively. My paper addresses this problem.

Limitations of Past Techniques

Many ESL teachers, having adopted the communicative approach to language teaching, ask me if pronunciation can also be taught in a way that is compatible with the communicative approach. My response is that it can be, but not by applying only the following techniques from the past (which have never yielded very good results):

1. Listen and repeat (a technique from the direct method).

2. Tongue twisters (a technique from L_1 speech correction); for example, She sells sea shells by the seashore.

3. Minimal pairs (a technique from audio-lingualism); for example, words: rice/lice; syntagmatic sentences: Don't *sit* on that *seat*; paradigmatic sentences: Don't (slip, sleep) on the floor.

4. Developmental approximation drills (a technique suggested by first language acquisition studies):

$$/w/ \longrightarrow /r/ \qquad \text{wed} \longrightarrow \text{red}$$

$$/y/ \longrightarrow /l/ \qquad \text{yet} \longrightarrow \text{let}$$

5. Vowel shifts and stress shifts (a technique based on generative phonology):

vowel shift: B*i*ble ——➤ b*i*blical

stress shift: phótograph ——➤ photógraphy

While useful on a limited, individual basis for purposes of correction and drill, none of these exercise types is in tune with the communicative approach to language teaching. The material they employ is artificial and unauthentic. With the focus on isolated words and/or sentences, there is little transfer from practice to natural communication. The structured and analytic nature of these drills also makes them extremely unmotivating.

A Communicative Approach to Teaching Pronunciation

The communicative approach presents language through tasks that focus on meaning, using activities such as role playing, problem solving, and games. Can we use such an approach if we want to teach pronunciation rather than grammar points, functions, or vocabulary? I believe we can, and some example activities that I have used successfully follow.

/θ/ and /ð/

The first set of exercises contains some of the activities I have developed as I have applied this strategy to the teaching of the two *th* sounds in English (voiceless /θ/ and voiced /ð/), which do not lend themselves well to practice with minimal pairs.

I have used body parts to focus initially on /θ/: mouth, tooth/teeth, throat, thumb, and thigh. The practice activity involves a brief role play between a doctor or a dentist, and a patient. The student playing the patient receives a card with a drawing of the body part that hurts, and the other student receives a card with commands that cue the questions the doctor should ask the patient (e.g., "Find out what's wrong.").

> Doctor: What's wrong?
> Patient: My throat hurts.
> Doctor: How long has it hurt you?

A few sessions later I used a calendar for the current month as a context for again practicing /θ/ in numbers with 3, ordinals, and in the words *Thursday* and *month*. (The circled days will receive special emphasis.)

		April		1987		
S	M	Tu	W	Th	F	S
			1	(2)	(3)	4
5	6	7	8	(9)	10	11
12	(13)	14	(15)	(16)	17	18
19	20	21	22	(23)	24	25
26	27	28	29	(30)		

For pair work, one student has the calendar for the month while the other has written cues for questions he or she must address to the student with the calendar.

> 1. Number of days (this, last, next) month?
> 2. Date of the first Friday?
> 3. Date of the second Monday?
> 4. Date taxes are due in the U.S.?
> 5. 13th on a Friday?

A few sessions later, to focus on /ð/, I use kinship terms since many of the common ones have this sound with *sister* being the major exception: (grand) mother, (grand) father, brother (-in-law), and sister (-in-law).

Practice can be done in groups of four or five. One student with a large family will answer questions while the others will ask at least two questions each by drawing on the eight kinship terms; the questions should be original, and the responses true.

Cards	Questions	Responses
grandfather	Is your grandfather alive?	Yes.
mother	What's your mother's name?	Olivia.
brother	Do you have any brothers?	Yes, two.

Perhaps two more class sessions will pass before I introduce a final exercise in this series. The final exercise consists of a family tree that combines the above kinship terms which focus on /ð/, with proper English names that focus on /θ/: the Thorpe family—Beth, Arthur, Ruth, Garth, Martha, Theodore, Dorothy, and Keith.

The students then work in pairs. Each one has a partial Thorpe family tree and must complete his or her tree by eliciting the appropriate information from his or her partner:

> Who is Garth's mother?
> Who is Martha's brother?

/iy/ and /ɪ/

Applying similar activities to a problematic vowel contrast (i.e., /iy/, /ɪ/), I begin with a sketch of a man with arrows pointing to the following body parts, which allow me to focus on the /ɪ/ sound: finger, lips, wrist, chin, ribs, hips, and shin. In pairs or groups the students develop a short dialog involving each of these body parts; then each pair/group presents one of its dialogs to the class.

> A: Bob is mad because he hurt his finger.
> B: How do you know he hurt his finger?
> C: Because he told me.

To focus on the contrasting /iy/ sound, we take a trip to the zoo with pictures. The animals of interest are: the zebra, the seal, the cheetah, the emu, the peacock, and the beaver. In groups of six, each group with a small set of six pictures to share, the students do a cumulative chain drill for initial practice:

> S 1: We went to the zoo and saw a zebra.
> S 2: We went to the zoo and saw a zebra and a seal.
> S 3: We went to the zoo and saw a zebra, and a seal, and
>   an emu.

In pairs they then work with complementary maps to locate the animals in the zoo at places such as the stream, the palm tree, and the peanut stand.

A few sessions later the class will integrate practice of /iy/ versus

/I/ using a role-playing situation involving a customer and a waiter or waitress in a restaurant. Each participant receives a copy of the menu. Typical questions are reviewed before the role play starts.

> What would you like first?
> What will you have next?
> Which vegetable?
> And for your dessert?

One student plays the customer, the other the waiter or waitress. To check for accuracy of communication, each partner circles the items ordered. After the role play has been completed, the partners should compare their menus to be sure they have circled the same items.

Dinner Menu

First Course:

Chicken Soup OR Fish Salad

Main Course:

Liver OR Veal OR Beef

Vegetable:

Peas OR Beans OR Spinach

Salad:

Green OR Mixed

Dessert:

Cheesecake OR Ice Cream OR
Mint Sherbet

Beverages:

Tea OR Milk OR Mineral Water

Development of Activities

There are a very few published references that assist the interested EFL teacher with ideas for such communicative exercises. Other than my own work (Celce-Murcia, 1983a, b), I can recommend only a few sources such as Hecht and Ryan (1979) and Pica (1984). For teachers who want to develop their own drills, teaching pronunciation communicatively involves the following steps:

1. Identify your students' problem areas (different groups of students may have different problems).

2. Find lexical/grammatical contexts with many natural occurrences of the problem sound(s).

3. Develop communicative tasks that incorporate the word.

4. Develop at least three or four exercises so that you can recycle the problem and keep practicing the target sound(s) with new contexts.

In other words, the same types of activities used to teach other language areas communicatively can also be used to teach pronunciation.

Concluding Remarks

I do not want to leave the reader with the impression that the traditional techniques are never applicable. On a limited, individual basis, it may in fact be useful for a teacher to assign manipulative drills to a well-motivated student who cannot master a given sound or contrast despite the use of communicative exercises. For such students, individual work with minimal pairs, tongue twisters, or successive approximation drills may still be a necessary and useful supplement. The point I wish to emphasize here is that I do not feel that instruction should begin with such drills; however, I feel teachers should still use them selectively when necessary and with those individuals who want and need such exercises. In certain cases, articulatory explanations of sounds can also be useful, but they should likewise be used on a selective basis and not presented as a lecture to the entire class.

In addition to the use of communicative activities, I try to vary classroom practice so that my students do not get bored or lose interest. I have found that practicing and reciting manageable segments of poetry, light verse, or song lyrics[4], that reinforce sounds we have practiced, can frequently serve this purpose. "The Eagle" by Alfred Lord Tennyson and "The Turtle" by Ogden Nash are examples of selections I have used in this way. Another excellent and even more authentic type of practice can be carried out using carefully selected excerpts from plays. My colleague Clifford Prator, who first made me aware of the great potential that play reading offers for teaching pronunciation, has often used excerpts from Thornton Wilder's *Our Town*. I prefer using excerpts from *The Odd Couple* by Neil Simon, but my motivation for using such material is identical to Prator's: Give students a chance to read aloud or even act out whole chunks of dramatic conversation where they have to use the stress, intonation, and phrasing appropriate to a given character in a given situation. This is pronunciation practice at its most demanding — something that can be challenging even for native speakers.

A caveat I must include in this discussion is that I do not feel students should have to worry about pronunciation at the very beginning stage of learning English. Research in first and second language acquisition suggests that initial teaching priorities for language areas should be vocabulary, grammar, and pronunciation — in that order. For literate students there is no particular skill order other than practice in listening comprehension should precede any of the other three skills (speaking, reading, writing).

The one glaring omission in my current approach is that I am still having problems with fully integrating stress and intonation into my teaching of English pronunciation. Linguists have recently made important contributions to the analysis of stress and intonation (see Gunter, 1974; Brazil, Coulthard, & Johns, 1980). Some very good techniques such as those suggested by Allen (1971) have been available to us for some time now. I use their suggestions, yet am not satisfied with the results. This is an area that I and other teachers must continue to work with and improve.[5] However, the fact that the focus of my pronunciation instruction now very explicitly centers on communication rather than manipulation means that I can also indirectly encourage practice of appropriate stress and intonation through modeling and individual correction. Certainly, my students have shown me that their pronunciation improves far more from doing these kinds of communicative activities than it ever did while they were doing only the the old techniques I listed in the second part of this paper. Such results are reason enough for me to believe that I am on the right track and to encourage you to use similar techniques.

Footnotes

[1]I wish to point out that the exercises used as illustrations in this paper have been designed to practice American rather than British pronunciation.

[2]This device reached its most sophisticated and usable form in the contextualized minimal pair drills of Bowen (1972, 1975). For example, *The blacksmith (hits, heats) the horseshoe (with the hammer, in the fire).* However, even such contextualized drills are not natural enough for learners to automatically incorporate what they learn into their everyday conversations in English.

[3]Note that I do not suggest that the goal of teaching pronunciation should be to make the learner sound like a native speaker of English. With the exception of a few highly gifted and motivated individuals, such a goal is completely unrealistic anyway. The more modest goal I have in mind is that of enabling learners to get above the threshold level so that the quality of their pronunciation will not inhibit their ability to communicate.

[4]I would like to stress that song lyrics should be spoken and not sung if pronunciation practice is the objective. Singing distorts the sound of spoken words and phrases, of stress and intonation, thereby detracting from any pedagogical value the exercise might otherwise offer for pronunciation practice.

[5]There is, for example, some good reinforcement activity available in many of the poems of Christina Rosetti. Her poems often include many questions and answers and thus provide opportunity for intonation practice.

References

Allen, V. F. (1971). Teaching intonation: From theory to practice. *TESOL Quarterly,* 5(1), 73-81.

Bowen, J. D. (1972). Contextualizing pronunciation practice in the ESOL classroom. *TESOL Quarterly,* 6(1), 83-94.

Bowen, J. D. (1975). *Patterns of English pronunciation.* Rowley, MA: Newbury House.

Brazil, D., Coulthard, M., & Johns, C. (1980). *Discourse intonation and language teaching.* London: Longman.

Celce-Murcia, M. (1983a). Teaching pronunciation communicatively. *MEXTESOL Journal,* 7(1), 10-25.

Celce-Murcia, M. (1983b, May). Activities for teaching pronunciation communicatively. *CATESOL Newsletter,* pp. 10-11.

Gunter, R. (1974). *Sentences in dialog.* Columbia, SC: Horbeam.

Hecht, E., & Ryan, G. (1979). *Survival pronunciation: Vowel contrasts* (Teacher's guide and student workbook). Hayward, CA: Alemany.

Hinofotis, F., & Bailey, K. (1980). American undergraduates' reactions to the communication skills of foreign teaching assistants. In J. C. Fisher, M. A. Clarke, & J. Schacter (Eds.), *On TESOL '80* (pp. 120-133). Washington, DC: Teachers of English to Speakers of Other Languages.

Pica, T. (1984). Pronunciation activities with an accent on communication. *English Teaching Forum,* 22(3), 2-6.

Scovel, T. (1969). Foreign accents: Language acquisition and cerebral dominance. *Language Learning,* 19(3 & 4), 245-254.

Learner Variables and Prepronunciation Considerations in Teaching Pronunciation

Rita Wong

San Francisco State University

Editorial Notes

In "Learner Variables and Prepronunciation Considerations in Teaching Pronunciation" Rita Wong focuses our attention squarely on the learner and urges us not to dismiss pronunciation instruction as ineffective, without making the kinds of modifications in our teaching practices which take the learner's perspective into account. She notes that an emphasis on pronunciation instruction that has centered on mastering the sounds of English, apart from the role they play in communication, has made it difficult for students to see the relevance of class work to communicative demands outside the classroom.

In the first part of the paper, Wong suggests that an initial step in planning instruction is to take a careful look at the students' backgrounds and experiences in language learning, and to move from there to establishing common goals, planning a systematic approach, and analyzing initial speech samples as a base for monitoring progress. In the second part of the paper, she carefully outlines the procedures for several very useful communicative activities which she recommends as prepronunciation work. She feels that such preparatory work can be instrumental in helping students understand the need for clarity as communicators from their own experience, not from the teacher's wise pronouncements.

Developing active listening skills. In using communicative activities in the classroom, teachers sometimes discover that students do not listen to each other. This is an obstacle to communication that must be overcome before students can begin to focus on pronunciation in communicative contexts. One activity outlined by Wong is called *active-listening-and-attending,* which has its roots in counseling training and was first applied to ESL teaching by Cope and Acton (1978). The main purposes of the activity are (a) to teach students how to show that they are listening and (b) to demonstrate how they can take control when they do not understand what someone is saying. Overall, it establishes a common foundation for the class' understanding of what it means to communicate. Another activity outlined is the familiar "strip story," a version of a scrambled sentence exercise first described by Gibson (1975). This is a compelling activity in which students find themselves in the positions of both rapt listeners to other students, as well as speakers with very attentive listeners.

Developing a comfortable level of fluency. Wong feels that in addition to good listening skills, students should have experience in communicating with other students before focusing on the specifics of pronunciation. *The fluency workshop,* an activity developed by Maurice (1983), gives students the chance to talk about the same topic to three different listeners consecutively, but with a decreasing amount of time allotted for each successive round. *The discussion* is suggested as a format which provides students with the opportunity to communicate with more than one other person at a time, and gives them experiences in playing the roles of discussion leader and discussion reporter, as well as discussion participant.

Wong suggests that if students are to appreciate the relevance of pronunciation to real-life communication, it is essential for them to understand the need for clarity as communicators. She recommends prepronunciation work of the kind described above to help students recognize when and how pronunciation can obscure communicative clarity.

J.M.

Learner Variables and Prepronunciation Considerations in Teaching Pronunciation

The teaching of pronunciation is not exclusively a linguistic matter. Yet, it has appeared that concerns about how to teach students to pronounce English and, indeed, whether or not pronunciation is teachable have overshadowed other factors, which have an equal bearing on the outcome of this endeavor. One of the major factors we seem to have overlooked is the learner and how not only the native language, but also personality and history of learning experiences (including experience of language learning) affect a learner's expectations of what and how to learn. Certainly, a learner's objectives for language learning will influence how he or she may view the importance of pronunciation. Moreover, the fact that pronunciation instruction has placed greater emphasis on mastering the sounds of English, apart from the role they play in communication, has made it difficult for many learners to see the relevance of class work to communicative demands outside of the classroom. It would be premature to dismiss pronunciation instruction as ineffective without making the kinds of modifications in our teaching practices which take the learner's perspective into account.

Who Are Our Students?

Before we launch into our lesson, we need to take a careful look at who our students are. What native languages do they speak, and what are some general characteristics of these languages? Have they learned English from teachers who speak it nonnatively? How much exposure to authentic spoken English have they had? Have they learned English primarily through reading it and discussing its grammar in their native languages? What experiences of using English for communication have the students had? How do they feel about learning and speaking English: excited, bored, fearful, fearless? How skillful are they as listeners?

Knowing something about students' native languages is helpful, not for the purpose of predicting what might be difficult for learners, but more importantly for helping us understand patterns of oral language behavior. For example, why does one student omit consonants at the ends of words? Why does another pronounce every syllable with equal time? It will help us be more patient with errors, which may not be the result of poor scholarship but, in fact, may be typical characteristics of norms in their native language.

Chances are that many of the students have learned English without hearing it spoken natively. What may be most helpful to them, initially, is to have the opportunity to listen to spoken English in order to get a general feeling of the way English sounds: the way words run into each other, the rhythm of speech, and the rises and falls in pitch within sentences. Here it is important to point out that the kind of spoken English I am describing is spoken English as it is used in communication, not as it is created to demonstrate the structure of English.

Students who have had minimal (or no) experience using English as a form of communication need to begin, not with pronunciation exercises, but with communicative experiences. In doing so, they can begin to develop some fluency and learn how to modify their speech in order to be more intelligible to their listeners. Some students are so afraid of speaking that they seem perpetually tongue-tied. Others carry on with unabashed fluency but to uncomprehending listeners. By providing a setting in which communication is the object, the tongue-tied student can become motivated to speak, and the fluent but incomprehensible student can learn to be clearer. When students can correct themselves without teacher intervention, given that they know that they have not communicated successfully, it is preferable that they do so.

The average learner needs to learn effective listening skills: how to listen and what to listen for. Students who are skillful listeners are likely to be skillful speakers; if not, they often quickly learn to be skillful speakers.

A student in a constant state of fear or one who is bored is not going to make much progress with pronunciation. A relaxed, supportive classroom environment in which students are comfortable with the teacher and with each other is essential. Creating such an environment depends largely on the teacher's ability to help students learn to respect each other, to identify reasonable objectives for the students to meet, to help the students meet these objectives, to be understanding when the process may take longer than expected, and to make the classroom experience pleasant and profitable. Even the least motivated student will respond if the classroom experience is enjoyable. Once the student's interest has been piqued, sustaining that interest will depend on the teacher's ability to demonstrate the relevance of pronunciation work to the student's personal objectives.

Establishing Common Goals

1. Intelligible Pronunciation for Communicative Effectiveness

Typically, students, and sometimes teachers, have an unreasonable goal: to achieve mastery over the pronunciation system. While complete mastery is unrealistic, intelligibility is attainable and desirable. However, many learners, especially young adults, have little idea of their own intelligibility. It is not until they are placed in a situation in which they are accountable for their communicative skills that they become aware of their performance. Many foreign teaching assistants and nonnative speakers in the workplace are examples of learners who must now face the fact that they are not intelligible enough. As teachers, we must try to create the kind of environment in our classrooms which allows students to recognize when they are unintelligible. We must help the student reach the standards of intelligibility by *not* understanding them when others outside of the classroom do not. We need to make a conscious effort to turn off our internal second language translators and make students more responsible for making themselves understood. Another way to approach this problem is to design field assignments which require students to communicate with native speakers in the community. Within the classroom we can also teach students to let each other know when they do not understand. How often have students listened in uncomprehending silence as a fellow student spoke unintelligibly?

While it is a significant step for students to recognize feedback cues which tell them that they are not communicating successfully, they also need to know how to locate the source of the problem. Pronunciation instruction can show students what the major features of the spoken English system are, and how they contribute to the expression of meaning and to communication in general. It can teach students how to perceive these features in natural speech as a preliminary step to perceiving these features in their own speech. This skill is especially important in view of the fact that we cannot describe the myriad features of natural speech in sufficient detail to teach them to students. What we can reasonably do is teach students what and how to perceive speech phenomena for themselves. Pronunciation instruction cannot realistically alter students' speech to become more English-like; it can only provide students with the tools to do so, if they want to.

2. Monitoring Progress

Unless learners know what they can reasonably achieve in a semester or a quarter year of work, it will be difficult for them, as well as for their teachers, to evaluate their progress. Without a sense of making progress, learners can easily become discouraged.

Planning a Systematic Approach

A systematic approach emphasizes relationships among the parts of the system, for example, the connection between syllables and rhythmic patterns; as a result, attention to one part supports the development of another. By identifying the key elements of the system, teaching priorities can be established, those that play critical roles receiving more attention than those that play lesser roles. On the basis of the overall system and the learner's individual needs and goals, the teacher can begin to plan the syllabus. An unsystematic approach has rarely made an impact on learners; for example, one or two lessons on the pronunciation of final *s* or *ed*, or lessons focused exclusively on so-called reduced forms, only contribute to the feeling that pronunciation teaching is ineffective. A systematic approach also enables learners to acquire gradually a sct of tools which will assist them in evaluating their own progress, a necessary ability if learners are to continue developing beyond the classroom.

Getting to Know Our Students

Planning an activity, such as an "icebreaker" game which offers opportunities for class members to begin talking to each other, is an effective way to start the course. After this initial interactional activity, a more in-depth type of activity, such as having students interview each other to find common experiences, will help students become better acquainted and more comfortable with each other. These activities also allow the teacher to form some general impressions of the students' abilities to communicate.

Within the first week of the course, the teacher should arrange to meet with each student on an individual basis to try to collect more specific data about the student's backgrounds and goals, as well as a sample of the student's speech. The teacher can use this taped speech sample to analyze the student's pronunciation and to determine the areas of emphasis for the class. At the end of the class the tape provides a measure for comparison. While this activity is time consuming, especially with large classes, its impact on the students is well worth the time and effort. The individual contact tells the student that the teacher is concerned and knows something about his or her strengths and weaknesses. Having this individual profile of the student will also help the teacher avoid treating the students as an undifferentiated group. The initial and final tapings provide a measure of progress, which is difficult to make concrete to students, where pronunciation is concerned.

Tips on Taking Initial Speech Samples[1]

1. Get a uniform sample from each student. Having students read the same text produces this uniformity and simplifies the job of tape analysis. While some samples may be confounded by students' reading difficulties, the comparative simplicity of evaluating readings of a uniform text may be preferable to analyzing more open-ended tasks, such as asking students to describe a picture or series of pictures, respond to a series of questions, or solve a problem with another student.

2. Keep the taped sample short, about 3-4 minutes.

3. Choose a text that comes from material you plan to use in the course; the text should be about the students' level, and you can get an advance idea of how they handle the material.

4. Do not try to analyze everything. Make your choices on the basis of your students' objectives and what you feel should be high priority based on those objectives: rhythmic patterns, incorrectly stressed syllables, incorrectly accented words, lack of linking, omission of final consonant sounds, and consonant clusters.

5. Report the results of your analyses to your students in individual conferences or in writing, depending on your time constraints.

Providing Focused Listening Opportunities

Exposure to spoken English is important for pronunciation development but exposure alone does not guarantee results. For many learners it is focused listening that makes a difference. In planning the syllabus, care should be taken to provide sufficient samples of spoken English that meet the following criteria:

1. Samples should include texts which go beyond the sentence level.

2. Samples should include a range of participant roles: discourse among peers, among speakers of the same and opposite sex, among speakers of different ages, and among speakers of different levels of authority.

3. Where possible, authentic speech should be included. The students' proficiency level is a determinant of the appropriateness of using authentic speech. If simplified or teacher prepared language is used, it should be spoken as naturally as possible and not distorted for the sake of artificial clarity.

The language classroom should be examined to determine to what extent supplementary language data must be supplied. Some classrooms are language rich, while others are language poor. An example of a language rich class is one in which students hear a variety of speakers engaged in diverse communicative events. A language poor classroom is one in which the student listens only to the teacher interacting with them as a teacher on classroom topics and tasks. Many sources of speech samples are available for pronunciation work: (a) commercially prepared tapes and videotapes which accompany grammar or listening comprehension texts; (b) radio programs, such as National Public Radio's "All Things Considered," or Canadian Broadcasting Company's "As it Happens," and "Soundings"; (c) recordings of books; (d) tapes of lectures, for example, National Press Club, Commonwealth Club, videotapes of television programs, plays, and films.

These sources provide the context which will help illustrate how features of pronunciation function in speech. The degree to which you can analyze these texts will depend on your own training and experience. If you are new to teaching pronunciation, you might settle for providing regular listening opportunities until you have acquired enough skills to give your students more specific guidelines and feedback.

Developing Active Listening Skills and a
Comfortable Level of Fluency

Although communication has been the tacit goal of language learning for a long time, language instruction has rarely resembled the kind of communication that takes place beyond the classroom walls; exercises have not required students to talk to or to understand each other. Now, in introducing communicative activities into the classroom, teachers have sometimes discovered that students do not listen to each other. Many students have said that they cannot understand other nonnative speakers of English, and they feel that to listen to them would adversely affect their own pronunciation. This initial obstacle to communication has to be overcome before students can begin to focus on pronunciation in communicative contexts. In preparation for this kind of pronunciation work, students must first learn how to be effective listeners and speakers.

1. Effective Listening Activities

(a) The strip story.

A version of a scrambled sentence activity, the strip story procedure as described by Gibson (1975), makes listening to one another a
necessary and urgent matter. Each student is given, at random, a
strip of paper on which one sentence of a story (any kind of cohesive
text) has been written. The students are instructed to memorize their
sentences and turn their strips over on their desks. Their task is to
reconstruct the story. As each student has a unique and essential
piece of information, it is important for the group to understand every
one. Sometimes it may be necessary for a student to repeat a sentence
several times, until the class is satisfied that they understand it. It is
not unusual for a student's pronunciation to improve with each repetition. Students find themselves in the positions of being both rapt
listeners to other students, as well as speakers with attentive listeners.

(b) Active-listening-and-attending.

This activity has its roots in counseling training. Its application to
ESL teaching was first suggested by Cope and Acton in 1978 at the
TESOL Convention, subsequently adapted by Chan and Underdal
(1983), and further adapted in the procedure described below. The
main purpose of this activity, in addition to teaching students how to
show that they are listening, is to demonstrate how they can take
control when they do not understand what someone is saying.
1. First explain that in a communicative event, there is at least one
speaker and one listener, and that both affect the success of that
event. If listeners do not show that they are listening, speakers may
not be interested in continuing to talk. If listeners fail to understand
the speaker, they have a responsibility to ask for repetition or clarification. You are going to demonstrate an exercise which will help the
class focus on the listener's important role in communication. After
the demonstration, the rest of the class will have an opportunity to
take part.
2. Ask for a volunteer to come up to the front of the classroom and
talk to you about a topic for 3 minutes. You will demonstrate listening
behavior while the volunteer speaks. Ask the class to focus on you,
and to observe and record what you do as a listener to show that you
are listening. You might ask the students to predict the kinds of
behavior that they might see: for example, eye contact; listening
sounds such as "uh-huh," "mmhmm"; words such as "yes," "yeah,"
"oh?" "really?"; and phrases asking for repetition and clarification.
Try to be as natural as you can and avoid exaggerating by using more
listening behavior than normal.
3. At the end of 3 minutes, ask the class to enumerate what they
observed. Ask the speaker to describe his or her feelings about your

listening behavior and how the class might have encouraged him or
her to speak.

4. Now divide the class into groups of three, assigning each to one
of the roles of listener, speaker, and observer. Suggest a couple of
possible topics for the speaker to talk about. For example, describe
your living accommodations, your trip to the U.S., or your current
job. Instruct the listeners to try to be cooperative, to be attentive, to
help the speaker by asking questions on the topic if the speaker
seems to be at a sudden loss for words, but not to take over the
talking. The observer should take notes of the listener's behavior and
be ready to report on it to the small group when the speaker has
finished talking. Allow 5 minutes for this part of the activity: 3
minutes for the speaker, 2 minutes for the observer to report.

5. Ask one or two observers to summarize their observations for
the large group. Then have the students switch roles. The observer
becomes the listener, the listener becomes the speaker, and the
speaker becomes the observer. Follow the steps outlined in #4.

6. For the final round, instruct the students to switch roles once
again. The observer will become the listener, the listener becomes
the speaker, and the speaker becomes the observer.

7. After the students have played all three roles, spend about
10-15 minutes summarizing their observations of the activity. Start
by making a master list of the ways listeners demonstrated effective
listening skills. Then ask how the speakers felt. You might add these
observations: (a) The effective listener can obtain information from a
speaker, even when the speaker may not be clear, by using good
listening techniques, for example, asking for clarification; and (b)
speakers can learn to be better speakers by being attentive to what
listeners tell you they understand or do not understand.

The activity establishes a common foundation for the class' understanding of what it means to communicate. However, as the teacher,
you need to assist the students by showing them when to employ
these techniques. Many students feel it is more polite to listen without understanding than to interrupt and get clarification. They need
to be shown how to interrupt acceptably. The total time for this
exercise, including the demonstration, is 45-50 minutes.

2. Developing a Comfortable Level of Fluency

In addition to good listening skills, students should have some
experience in communicating with other students before focusing on
the specifics of pronunciation. This experience is beneficial for all
students, especially those who lack communicative experiences or are
unable to assess their degree of communicative clarity. Two kinds

of activities can be used for this purpose, the fluency workshop and the discussion.

(a) The fluency workshop.

This activity, developed by Maurice (1983), will loosen the tongue of the most tongue-tied student. It is a very low risk speaking task since it involves speaking to only one other person at a time; and as everyone is occupied, no one else is listening in on the conversation. Here is how it can be set up.[2] The purpose of this activity is to give students the chance to talk about the same topic but to three different listeners consecutively. They are given decreasing periods of time for each round with the longest period for the first round. With each subsequent round, the speakers become more familiar with what they want to say and can say it more fluently.

1. Ask the students to sit or stand in a large circle. (The first time it might be easier to have the students seated since the chairs help to identify locations when the students change partners.)

2. Explain the purpose of the activity, that is, to develop their oral fluency by giving them three opportunities to talk about the same topic.

3. Explain the procedure. Pair students off, and label one A and the other B. The A's will begin as speakers; the B's will begin as listeners. There will be three rounds. The first round will be 4 minutes long. Then the A's will move one person to the right and speak on the same topic with a new partner for 2 minutes. For the third round, the A's will again move one person to the right and speak for 1 minute. (The times can be varied, but as an introduction to the exercise, shorter times work best.) The listeners should be reminded to use active listening behavior. They may ask questions to help the speaker continue speaking, but should not take over. Tell the listener that you will be asking them to report on what they heard at some point. After the A's have completed three rounds, the B's will become speakers and the A's will become listeners. The A's will continue nevertheless to move to new partners. Be sure the students understand what to do before you ask them to begin.

4. Give the speakers a topic. Tell the B's that they will have different topics, or they might try to use their listening time to prepare for their turn.

5. Begin the exercise. It will be noisy, as half the class will be speaking simultaneously. It is a buzz that warms the hearts of teachers who want to encourage students to speak, but neighboring classes may not share the same enthusiasm, so make appropriate arrangements.

6. After the A's have finished, you might ask a few B's to report on what they heard. Then give the B's their topic.

7. After the B's have finished, ask some of the A's to report on what they heard.

8. When both A's and B's have concluded their three turns each, ask students to discuss any differences they could detect between the first and third rounds. They will generally say that it was easier for them to talk about the same thing on the third try.

Allow 50 minutes for this exercise. This activity can be used as many times as the class likes during the course.

(b) The discussion.

The discussion format provides students with the opportunity to communicate with more than one other student. However, as many students are inexperienced with discussions, it helps to begin first with an orientation to some of the purposes of discussions and to the roles of participants. Students can integrate what they have learned about active listening as participants and help each other as they attempt to communicate with each other on topics in which, ideally, they are interested.

Here is a suggested procedure for introducing discussions:

1. Decide on a suitable topic for your students. (This is where knowing something about them helps.)

2. Determine the composition and size of each group. Aim for heterogeneity of language backgrounds, personalities, and language abilities. Groups of between four and six students work well. As students warm up to discussions and the composition of each group is of less significance, an easier and faster way to divide students up is to count them off by fours if you want four groups, fives if you want five, and so forth. Other ways to divide students are: early risers/late sleepers; oldest/middle one/youngest in a family; or those who wear glasses and those who do not.

3. Assign and explain the roles of participants in a discussion. These roles have been prescribed in order to teach students about discussions, since many have not had experience with them.

a. The discussion leader is responsible for introducing the topic and making sure that everyone understands it. Assuring everyone in the group of a chance to speak, the leader guards that no one monopolizes the discussion and encourages the reticent students to contribute.

b. The reporter takes notes of what participants say during the discussion and summarizes these comments for the larger group at the conclusion of the small group discussion. The reporter also participates in the discussion.

c. The participants listen actively by asking for clarification, checking for understanding, and adding comments to the topic.

4. Establish a time limit for the small group discussions, and make sure everyone knows what that time limit is.

5. Check to be sure that the group leader understands what the topic is.

6. When time is up, listen to the reports from each group. Plan the class hour so that there is time for this part of the discussion exercise.

7. Comment on the way the discussions were carried out, as well as on the reports. What you comment on will depend on the objectives of this particular discussion.

During the discussion the teacher can circulate among the groups, listening and participating only when asked and then only to answer specific questions briefly. Keep in mind that the discussion exercise is an opportunity for the students to speak.

Final Note

The strip story, the activity listening exercise, the fluency workshop, and the discussion are examples of the kinds of activities that are recommended as prepronunciation work. Such preparatory work can be instrumental in helping students understand the need for clarity as communicators from experience, which is essential if they are to see the relevance of pronunciation work. As these exercises also sharpen their skills as listeners, they will be better equipped to benefit from communicative activities and to apprehend when pronunciation obscures communicative clarity. By placing greater emphasis on learner variables in pronunciation development than we have in the past, we should be able to see our students make the kind of progress that will be encouraging to them and to us.

References

Chan, M., & Underdal, K. (1983, April). *Teaching conversational listening skills.* Workshop conducted at the meeting of CATESOL, Los Angeles, CA.

Cope, C., & Acton, W. (1978, April). *Teaching conversational listening skills to ESL students.* Workshop conducted at the 12th Annual TESOL Convention, Mexico City.

Gibson, R. E. (1975). The strip story: A catalyst for communication. *TESOL Quarterly, 9,* 149-154.

Maurice, K. (1983). The fluency workshop. *TESOL Newsletter, 17*(4), p. 29.

Wong, R. (in press) *Teaching pronunciation: Focus on rhythm and intonation.* Washington, D.C.: Center for Applied Linguistics.

Footnotes

[1]For a more detailed discussion, see Wong (in press).

[2]I have adapted it slightly. For a description of the original format, see Maurice, 1983.

Pronunciation and Listening Comprehension

Judy B. Gilbert

Hayward, California

Editorial Notes

In the introduction to "Pronunciation and Listening Comprehension" Judy B. Gilbert takes up the theme that pronunciation and listening are related in a speech loop between speaker and listener. She feels that both skills can be improved by concentrating pronunciation class time on the systematic teaching of what she terms "the most powerful signals in spoken English": the intonational devices of pitch patterns and timing which form the musical patterns of English. She lists the most important functions of intonation as: (a) showing contrast between new information and old information, and (b) showing boundaries between thought groups.

She notes that these functions are critical to the discourse loop between speaker and listener because they keep clear what topics are important and how they interrelate. She suggests that because pitch patterns and timing are used in differing ways in different languages, English learners can be helped greatly by specific instruction in and practice of the main functions of English intonation and the basic physical devices: pitch change, lengthening, and vowel clarity. Similarly, practice with the signals for thought group boundaries can improve both comprehension and comprehensibility.

She develops these key points: (a) that comprehension is greatly affected by faulty musical patterns because these patterns are directly tied to critically important signals for meaning; (b) that if the students do not use these signals, pronunciation is impaired; and (c) that if the student does not recognize these signals in the speech of the native speaker, then comprehension is impaired. She believes that it is precisely in the teaching of the system of intonation that we can make the most productive use of pronunciation class time.

J.M.

Pronunciation and Listening Comprehension

Pronunciation and listening comprehension are related in a speech loop between speaker and listener. Both skills can be improved by concentrating pronunciation class time on the systematic teaching of the most important elements of pronunciation. The most powerful signals in spoken English are expressed by intonational devices: pitch patterns and timing. These elements form the musical patterns of English. The most important functions of intonation in English are:

(a) to show contrast between new information and old information, and
(b) to show boundaries between thought groups.

These functions are critical to the discourse loop between speaker and listener because they keep clear what topics are important and how they interrelate. Because pitch patterns and timing are used in different ways in different languages, English learners can be helped greatly by specific instruction in and practice of the main functions of English intonation and the basic physical devices: pitch change, lengthening, and vowel clarity. Similarly, practice with the signals for thought group boundaries can improve both comprehension and comprehensibility. By emphasizing these aspects of pronunciation, the teacher can convert the pronunciation class from a rote drill to a rewarding part of the ESL curriculum.

Relating Pronunciation and Listening Comprehension

How important are listening and pronunciation skills, and how much time should be allotted for them in a crowded curriculum? If you believe that language ability improves with communicative use, then listening and pronunciation are key elements. Conversation with native speakers typically comes to an embarrassed halt when the other person begins to find communication too difficult. This is the repeated experience of many of our students, and it is discouraging. Another source of discouragement comes when students fail to recognize spoken words which they know in reading. Few people realize that these two forms of difficulty are connected.

The speaker and the listener are connected through a speech loop of mutual comprehension in a continual process of reassessment. Communication depends on both sides following matching systems of speech signals. This is the reason that listening skills and pronunciation are directly interrelated. Furthermore, this interrelationship can be taught using rather simple building blocks. If the two skills are seen as a pair, then the pronunciation class can be restructured to integrate aspects of listening comprehension.

Consider this scene. The teacher has just completed a successful pronunciation lesson using minimal pairs of words to teach the sounds /r/ and /l/. All the students were able to manage the distinction by the end of the lesson. The students feel good, and the teacher feels good. Then, as the students are leaving the room, one turns to the teacher and says cheerily, "So rong!". The teacher no longer feels good.

Lack of success is discouraging to teachers, and students sometimes feel that pronunciation is an endless succession of unrelated and unmanageable pieces. This may be why the teaching of pronunciation has fallen into disfavor in so many programs. Instead of spending the bulk of our limited resources of time and energy on the practice of individual sounds, a more productive approach is to concentrate our efforts on the most powerful signals of meaning.

Intonation: The "Musical" Signals of English

In general, the most important part of English pronunciation is what might be referred to as the "music" of the language. This consists of basic elements of pitch patterns (melody) and timing patterns (rhythm). Each language uses these elements in distinctive ways which are learned at such an early age that the patterns become automatic. Since these musical patterns are unconsciously transferred to a new language, it is difficult for most second language learners to realize that they are speaking the new language with the music of the old language. If the only result of this transfer were to make a foreign accent, the problem would not be serious for most students.

In fact, the result is often severe loss of comprehensibility. Comprehension is greatly affected by faulty musical patterns because these patterns are directly tied to critically important signals for meaning. If the student does not use these signals, pronunciation is impaired. Similarly, if the student does not recognize these signals in the speech of a native speaker, then listening comprehension is impaired. It is precisely in the teaching of this system of musical signals that we can make the most productive use of pronunciation class time. In this paper, I will refer to these musical signals as *intonation*.

Brown (1977) explained the importance of intonation this way:

From the point of view of the comprehension of spoken English, the ability to identify stressed syllables and make intelligent guesses about the content of the message from this information is absolutely essential. (p. 52)

Marking New Information—Old Information

The most powerful principle our students can learn is this: English uses intonation to mark the distinction between old information and new information. Old information concerns ideas already discussed or mutually understood, and new information concerns the new thought to which the speaker wishes to call attention. Consider the following dialog:

> X: I've lost an *umbrella.*
> Y: A *lady's* umbrella?
> X: Yes, a lady's umbrella with *stars* on it. *Green* stars.
> (Allen, 1971, p.77)

In the first remark, X is calling attention to an umbrella. This is the focus of the remark. When Y answers, however, the umbrella is now understood to be the topic, and the new thought is expressed in the word *lady's.* A native speaker of English will therefore de-emphasize *umbrella* in order to highlight the word which is now the focus of meaning. Exactly the same process occurs in the next remark by X, since both *lady's* and *umbrella* are now mutually understood, and are therefore old information. The new focus is *stars.* This shift of emphasis is quite systematic in conversation because it helps the listener and speaker follow each other's thoughts. In a rough way, this kind of emphasis can be referred to as "sentence stress."

All languages have a systematic way of showing the distinction between new information and old, but English depends to an unusual extent on musical signals. This nearly unique dependence of English means that most of our students do not hear these signals naturally, and therefore can benefit greatly from explicit teaching.

Because sentence stress is so important in English, we have four different physical signals for it, to make absolutely sure that the listener notices. The four signals are: pitch change, length of vowel, clarity of vowel, and loudness.

The stress signal of loudness is more or less universal to human language as a marker of emphasis, and therefore teaching it has less effect than teaching the first three signals.

Figure 1. Summary: stressed syllable signals

1. *Pitch change*	record record economy economic
2. *Length*	atom atomic banana

3. *Clarity*
  a. Most unstressed vowels are clear.
  b. ALL STRESSED VOWELS ARE CLEAR.
	regïsTRAtïøn
	tø thé STAtïøn

From *Clear Speech* by J.B. Gilbert, 1984, New York: Cambridge University Press. Copyright 1984 by Cambridge University Press. Reprinted by permission.

Clarity of the vowel is a particularly difficult concept for many students since in their languages all vowels are spoken in a full, clear way. The English system of stress requires reduction of some vowels, because it is so important to show which syllables are stressed. Notice the vowel clarity contrasts in *atom* and *atomic*.

Contrast is the fundamental signalling principle. In speech, important words are emphasized, and less important words are systematically de-emphasized. It is common for language learners, in their desire to be understood, to emphasize many words in a sentence. This confuses the English listener, who depends on contrast of emphasis to know which words are genuinely important. We might compare this system of contrast with the visual contrast of a figure and its background. That is, the figure must stand out in some way in order to be perceived clearly. The background serves as a base line.

In English speech, the base line is a basic emphasis pattern. Changes from this base pattern are clear signals of emphasis to the listener who is familiar with the system. That is, efficient communication between the English speaker and the English listener requires the use of this system.

The basic emphasis pattern of English is fundamentally simple.

Figure 2.

BASIC EMPHASIS PATTERN			
CONTENT WORDS (emphasized)	*nouns,* (cat)	*main verbs,* (runs)	*adverbs,* (quickly) *adjectives* (happy)
STRUCTURE WORDS (not emphasized)	*pronouns,* (he, she)	*prepositions,* (of, to, at)	*articles,* (a, the) *"to be" verbs* (is, was)
	conjunctions, (and, but)	*auxiliary verbs* (can, have, do, will)	

Notice how the emphasis in the following limerick systematically distinguishes between content words and structure words:

> A *stu*dent was *sent* to Tacoma
> In*ten*ding to *earn* a di*plo*ma. He said, "With the *rain,*
> I don't *want* to re*main,*
> I *think* I'd pre*fer* Oklahoma."
> (Gilbert, 1984, p. 34)

The distinction between content and structure occurs in this "rhymalogue":

> Lee: I'll *meet* you at the *bank, Frank.*
> Frank: I'll *be* there at *three, Lee.*
> (Morley, 1979, p. 41)

The same basic emphasis pattern occurs in normal speech:

> I'll *meet* you at the *air*port in *Lon*don on *Fri*day. (Morley, 1979, p. 41).

Using this basic pattern as a base line, the speaker can draw attention to any word as a new focus of attention.

> I *will* meet you at the airport Sunday.
> X: Is it *on* the desk?
> Y: No, it's *in* the desk.

The speaker is making a deliberate choice, based on personal intent. Therefore, when students practice the distinction between old and new focus, they are working with language for real communication. Choose focus words for this dialogue:

A: What do you do for exercise?
B: Well, nothing, I guess.
A: You should, you know.
B: Yes, but I don't like it. (Gilbert, 1984, Quiz Six)

Thought Groups and Pause

Besides emphasizing focus words, musical signals are used to mark the end of thought groups. Notice how we typically group telephone numbers, in order to make them easier to understand: (213) 453-7852. The listener is aware of the grouping because the speaker marks the end of a group with a pause. In rapid speech there may not be time for a pause, so a second signal is relied on: a pitch fall on the final syllable. A falling pitch means "end." The greater the fall, the more final the signal. For instance, there is more of a pitch fall at the end of a sentence than at the end of a phrase. Naturally, the greatest fall is apt to occur at the end of a conversational turn. This is one way that the listener knows that it is now time to speak.

Algebraic equations or arithmetic problems can be used to practice hearing the pitch fall and pause which mark the end of a group. If you read these out loud, native speakers will "hear" the parentheses. Compare the following:

$$(A + B) \times C = X \ldots \ldots \ldots A + (B \times C) = X$$
$$(3 + 2) \times 4 = 20 \ldots \ldots \ldots 3 + (2 \times 4) = 11$$

In the same way, listeners can hear punctuation which marks thought groups:

(a) They like pie and apples.
(b) They like pineapples.

(a) "Alfred," said the boss, "is stupid."
(b) Alfred said, "The boss is stupid."

A group of British linguists studying discourse patterns explained the importance of intonation this way:

> Listening to phrasing . . . gives overt phonological marking to major constituents in sentence structure. . . thus intonation can assist the development of receptive skills and can help the student to process "what goes with what" and

how the information structure of a text develops.
(Brazil, Coulthard, & Johns, 1983, p. 131)

Final Notes

In summary, students can improve both speaking and listening by learning the musical signals of sentence stress and thought grouping. We can assist in their progress by systematically bringing pronunciation practice and listening comprehension together.

References

Allen, V. F. (1971). Teaching intonation, from theory to practice. *TESOL Quarterly*, 5(1), 73-81.

Brazil, D., Coulthard, M., & Johns, C. (1980). *Discourse intonation and language teaching.* London: Longman.

Brown, G. (1977). *Listening to spoken English.* London: Longman.

Gilbert, J. B. (1984). *Clear speech: Pronunciation and listening comprehension in American English.* New York: Cambridge.

Morley, J. (1979). *Improving spoken English.* Ann Arbor: The University of Michigan.

Pronunciation Tutorials for Nonnative Technical Professionals: A Program Description

Sandra C. Browne

General Motors Research Laboratories

Thomas N. Huckin

Carnegie-Mellon University

Editorial Notes

In "Pronunciation Tutorials for Nonnative Technical Professionals: A Program Description," Sandra C. Browne and Thomas N. Huckin describe a tutorial program in pronunciation/oral communication that they were asked to develop for a number of the foreign-born research scientists holding responsible positions in the General Motors Research Laboratories near Detroit. Although all of their clients had spoken English for many years and had resided in the United States for considerable lengths of time, each had a significant pronunciation/oral communication problem.

Analysis of the speech patterns of clients from 16 language backgrounds revealed four major problem areas which the authors addressed in their program:

1. Pronunciation of vowel sounds in stressed syllables with special attention to spelling/pronunciation confusions relating to English letter/sound correspondences.
2. Pronunciation of consonant sounds with special attention to consonant-to-consonant linking both within and across word boundaries.
3. Pronunciation of articles and grammatical suffixes, especially past tense and plural forms.
4. Rhythm, stress, and intonation in technical presentations.

The cognitive approach that Browne and Huckin have developed for their technical/professional research clientele is rated as highly effective by the participants in the program.

A central part of the Browne-Huckin program is helping students develop a three-part process of speech awareness, self-observation, and self-monitoring. In a unique part of their program, the tutors train their clients in strategies for analyzing their own manuscripts of the reports and papers they must present orally as part of their jobs. They are given instruction in analyzing text, picking out the most important words of the text for their purposes, and creating a rhythm pattern that puts stress on those words. Browne and Huckin use videotaping and critiquing in tutorial sessions and incorporate audiotaping in the self-study curriculum for their research professionals.

J.M.

Pronunciation Tutorials
for Nonnative Technical Professionals:
A Program Description

Forty-five foreign-born technical professional researchers at General Motors Research Laboratories (Warren, Michigan) participated in a series of 14, one-to-one tutorial programs with systematic follow-up over a period of 2 years. Sixteen language backgrounds were represented in this industrial research "student" population. Analysis of their speech patterns revealed four major problem areas impeding effectiveness in oral communication, particularly in the oral presentations of professional reports and papers demanded by their jobs. The four problems were: (a) pronunciation of vowels, including pronunciation/spelling confusions related to English sound/symbol correspondences; (b) pronunciation and linking of consonants, especially across word boundaries; (c) pronunciation of articles and grammatical suffixes, especially plural and past tense forms; and (d) rhythm and contrastive stress in technical presentations.

These problems were addressed beginning with a diagnostic analysis of each student's spoken English, followed by the designing of an individualized program using selected written and oral texts and materials. Extensive videotaping and audiotaping were used both in tutorial sessions and in the self-study curriculum.

Initial diagnostic testing and postcourse evaluation by the tutors corroborated observed improvements in individual speech patterns. In a separate management evaluation, these technical professional researchers rated the program as highly effective, and most of them elected to continue individual work in a follow-up, in-house program. Both students and tutors rated the cognitive approach which was employed as very effective and satisfying.

Program Description

Increasing numbers of foreign-born employees are being hired as technical professionals in American industry. Many of these nonnative speakers, though highly competent in technical skills, are deficient in communication skills of spoken English. Often this deficiency not only impedes day-to-day work within the company, but also hinders possibilities for advancement to managerial responsibility.

The technical professionals we tutor at General Motors Research Laboratories (GMR) are physicists, electrochemists, metallurgists, environmental scientists, biologists, psychologists, computer scientists, and transportation researchers. These technical researchers frequently must deliver formal oral reports in their areas of expertise. Because of the specialized nature of their work and their differing first language backgrounds, we have found one-to-one tutorial sessions to be the most effective mode of instruction (see Table 1 for language backgrounds of our participants).

Following initial diagnostic testing and speech analysis, work is assigned based upon assessment of performance skills in oral English. Due to the individualized nature of the instruction, no textbook is required for these sessions, but a variety of selected materials are used, including Morley (1979) and Morley (in press). Each participant is assigned an appointment time of 1 hour each week for a period of 14 weeks. Meetings are during working hours in the GMR Oral Communication Program Language Laboratory—a private room outfitted with dual-track audio tape recorders, video recording equipment, and a library of tapes especially prepared and adapted for this program. Participants are issued dual-track tape recorders for their personal use in preparing for the tutorial sessions, and are loaned tapes and materials each week as a portion of their homework assignment.

Table 1. *Language Backgrounds of GMR Oral Communication Program Participants*

Chinese	
(Cantonese, Mandarin, Taiwanese)	20
Indian	
(Hindi, Gujarati, Urdu, Tamil)	9
Korean	6
Japanese	2
Polish	2
Arabic	1
Croatian	1
Greek	1
Hebrew	1
Persian	1
Romanian	1

The Problem Areas

In the course of our work, we have identified four major problem areas in spoken English:

1. Articulation of vowel sounds in stressed syllables
2. Articulation and linking of consonant sounds
3. Use of determiners and inflected endings
4. Use of rhythm, stress, and intonation for discourse focus

Vowel Sounds

Difficulties in the articulation of vowel sounds in stressed syllables are a result, we believe, of a lack of attention in most English language instruction to the sound system of English. Moreover, even for students who must read papers and reports aloud, thus converting the written code to the spoken code, little instruction is given in spelling/sound relationships. The fact that written English has five vowel letters plus *y*, while spoken English uses 15 vowel sounds, is rarely addressed in English language classes. Attention is sometimes paid to the vagaries of the English spelling system, usually by use of a dictionary, but this dependence on the written code does not properly relate spoken sounds to the representations of these sounds in English. The letter *o*, for example, is but one of the five vowel letters in our written alphabet. But in spoken English the letter *o* is commonly pronounced as six different sounds in words as simple as *two, shop, no, dozen, software*, and *employ*. Here, learners of English as a second language who attempt to pronounce all written *o's* as /oᵂ/, relying upon the written code alone, are in trouble. Using materials Browne (1984) helped to develop, we give special attention to selected spelling/pronunciation correspondences of the English vowel system.

English vowel pronunciations, which differ markedly from those of the native speaker's first language, often require an introduction to articulatory differences in production for which tongue position, lip position, and jaw position serve as basic parameters. For example, speakers of languages like Mandarin Chinese, which has no low front vowel comparable to American English /æ/, *cat*, and no low back vowel (American English /ɔ/, *caught*), show that changes in tongue position produce *cat* rather than *cot* or *caught*.

Many of our participants have difficulty with long and short /u/ in pairs like *pool* and *pull, boot* and *book*. One of them jokingly told us that he had considered giving up his research on "soot particles" because he could not pronounce *soot* (i.e., it came out *suit*). In fact, his attention to the articulation of these two vowel sounds during his work with us led to significant improvement in his differential pronunciation of them. He no longer sounds like he is saying *suit particles* when he means *soot particles*. This participant found that once we had identified the underlying articulatory problem of slightly different tongue and lip positions for these two vowel sounds, he understood not only how to fix *soot* versus *suit*, but other problems of the same kind.

Another of our participants had great difficulty with /i/ in words like *seat* or *heat*, one of the problems familiar to ESL teachers. In attempting to pronounce *seat*, he would say *sit* instead, and for *heat* he would say *hit*. This pattern of mispronunciation proved to be most embarrassing when he gave an important oral presentation to upper management and found that throughout his 7-minute talk, when he tried to say *sheet metal*, it came out as something quite different, to everyone's chagrin.

Once the articulation of a vowel has been studied, both individually and in contrast to other vowels in the system, we explore sound/spelling correspondences. In the case of the letter *o*, only one of the six words mentioned above has the sound /o^w/. The spelling of that sound as the letter *o* occurs in two major patterns: (a) when the sound is in an open syllable, *no*; and (b) when *o* is followed by a single consonant plus a silent *e*, *code*. The frequency correlation for this particular sound/spelling correspondence is 87% (see Morley, 1979, p. 170). This means that when a word is written with *o* as its final letter or with *o* followed by a single consonant letter plus a silent *e*, the reader can safely assume that the correct pronunciation of the letter *o* is /o^w/. Exceptions to this correlation frequency of 87% are found in digraph spelling patterns as in words such as *slow*, *load*, *shoulder*, and *toe*, and in exceptions like *do*, *who*, and *po* (see Morley, in press, for more on pronunciation/spelling "safe rules").

GM research professionals learn that the written letter *o* can be pronounced in as many as 11 different ways, when followed by another vowel (as in *shout*). We also show them that sound/spelling correspondences work both ways. It is just as important to recognize that the letter *o* is not always pronounced /o^w/ as it is to learn spelling rules for *o* in monosyllabic words. For instance, the sound of the letter *o* when placed before *f* or *s* plus a second consonant (*soft*, *cost*) is pronounced /ɔ/ with even more regularity (96.85%) than in the case given above for *o* as /o^w/ in *code* (Hanna, Hanna, Hodges & Rudorf, 1966, p. 34). When *o* is pronounced as /a/ or /ə/ as in *stop* or *dozen*, spelling rules can be used to show which specific consonant letters pattern with each of these pronunciations (see Morley, 1985, for discussion).

We have found in the course of our teaching that the introduction of a one-to-one sound/symbol representation helps our participants better understand that although the sound/spelling correspondences of English are complicated, they are not hopelessly without pattern. The ability to use a dictionary, which has such a one-to-one representation of sounds to symbols, is a great advantage in second language teaching. We use the *Longman Dictionary of American English: A Dictionary for Learners of English* (1983) because it uses the sound symbols of the International Phonetic Alphabet for its pronunciation code. This permits our students to look up words like *oscillation*, *transformation*, and *obsolete* and find that none of them contains the sound /o^w/ for the letter *o*. We then explore aspects of vowel reduction in English.

Consonant Sounds

Many nonnative speakers have problems with the pronunciation of the /l/, /r/, /w/, /y/, /θ/, and /ð/ sounds in English, due to a combination of differences in both place and manner of articulation. English has consonant pairs which differ in manner of articulation (*nightlight*). A third source of difficulty may involve voicing. For example, /t/ and /d/ are both produced by placing the tongue-tip against the bony ridge just behind the upper teeth, but /t/ is *voiceless* (i.e., produced using air only), whereas /d/ is *voiced* (i.e., produced with vibration of the vocal cords). This difference in voicing together with vowel lengthening before voiced consonant sounds plays a crucial role in the pronunciation of past tense endings in English.

When native English speakers add *-ed* to a regular verb to indicate past tense, they automatically match the sound of the *-ed* to the final sound of the verb. For example, in *stop/stopped*, the final *-ed* is pronounced as /t/ to match the voiceless final /p/ sound in *stop*. If a verb ends in a voiced sound, like the /l/ in *call*, however, the *-ed* is pronounced as the sound /d/. The problem for the nonnative speaker is when to pronounce *-ed* as /t/ and when as /d/.

The simple rules for matching of voiced and voiceless sounds in English past tense, noun plurals, possessives, or third person singular verb forms can be illustrated in 15 minutes, once the principle of voicing is established as an essential feature of English pronunciation. Here again, pronunciation is often complicated by our spelling system. Languages such as Mandarin Chinese have nearly a one-to-one sound and spelling correspondence. For example, in Mandarin, the letter *d* is always pronounced [t], and the letter *t* is always pronounced [t^h]. Therefore, not only is there no voicing contrast in the pronunciation of these sounds (both are voiceless), but the Mandarin speaker has no way of knowing that the English letter *d* can have more than one pronunciation. It is not surprising, therefore, that Mandarin speakers tend to pronounce English verbs without past tense endings.

In addition to the use of voicing, as a major element of importance to intelligibility in spoken English, another equally important feature is the linking of consonants both within words and across word boundaries. Many languages of the world do not have clusters of three or even two consonant sounds without an intervening vowel sound. Therefore, words like *strike* and *risked* and *fifths* present problems for some nonnative speakers, as they attempt to insert a vowel sound between consonants. This vowel sound is often one that sounds like an American English "uh" [ʌ]. For example, in Polish the word for "poultry" is *drób,* /drup/. To American English speakers it is likely to sound like "duhroop," /dərup/, because of the vowel which regularly occurs between voiced consonants in Polish (Jassem, 1983, p. 123). Japanese speakers also use vowel sounds between consonant sounds in a pattern different from English. For a Japanese speaker the English word *stop* would not consist of one syllable, but three [sətopə].

Consonant clusters present the nonnative speaker with a complicated articulatory problem: How does one get from one consonant sound to another without introducing a vowel sound in between? In a word as complicated in its articulation as *fifths*, not only does learning the articulation of a nonnative sound like /θ/ require the repositioning of the tongue, but the contiguity of /θ/ with /s/ without an intervening vowel sound may demand an articulatory sequence foreign to the nonnative speaker's experience. One means of aiding the acquisition of these consonant articulations is to introduce the concept of juncture in order to highlight English consonant pronunciations and their patterns of lengthening and holding. For example, the two sentences below sound very much alike in casual speech:

1. He *must earn* more than 250,000 a year.
2. He *must turn* more than 250,000 a year.

While the first sentence clearly refers to money, the second could easily be overheard in a similar context and could refer (in the automotive industry) to the number of units a particular employee produces. The point is, the features of the juncture between *must earn* and *must turn* determine which meaning the sentence will have. For sentence 1. the final /t/ in *must* is released into the initial vowel sound in *earn*. In sentence 2. the final /t/ in *must* is held to indicate that the next word also begins with a /t/ sound. (For more examples of this type of consonant lengthening, see Morley, 1979, p. 51.) The importance of learning how sounds are connected is essential to good oral communication in English, because the listener needs these cues to interpret the meaning of the message.

Determiners and Inflected Endings

For many of our students the omission of determiners like *the* and *a*, and inflected endings like plural *-s* and past tense *-ed* constitutes a persistent problem. Instead of "First we want*ed* to measure *the* stress*es* to find *the* parameter*s* for friction allowance*s*," a nonnative speaker may say, "First we want to measure stress to find parameter for friction allowance."

Determiners and inflections are omitted by nonnative speakers for several reasons:

- They often do not have equivalents in the speaker's native languages (e.g., Korean, Chinese, Japanese), and so the speaker feels that they can be ignored in English as well.
- They do not carry as much obvious meaningful reference as nouns and verbs, and are felt by the nonnative speaker to be less important and therefore dispensible.
- They are difficult to use correctly, particularly definite articles which have a very complex use system.
- They may be difficult to pronounce. As discussed above, the /ð/ sound in *the* and the consonant clusters created by adding plural *-s* and past tense *-ed* to word forms which end in final consonants are typically not found in these speakers' native languages.

We attack these problems from several directions, but without departing from the cognitive approach that we and our students prefer. First, we point out that using correct grammar will enhance their image as well-educated professionals, and that is sufficient reason to use determiners and inflections correctly.

Second, we demonstrate how subtle differences of meaning can arise from the use or non-use of determiners and inflections. We argue that ignoring such differences leads to imprecision in one's speech. (As technical professionals, our students have a great respect for the importance of being precise.)

Third, we tell them that although the listener often can figure out what the speaker means, the listener should not be forced to perform the extra mental gymnastics that this requires. By omitting determiners and inflections, nonnative speakers put pressure on the listener, forcing the listener to pay closer attention than normal to the stream of speech. Although most native speakers find this irritating, students seem to be unaware of this. One student claimed, "I think my listeners want me to be concise."

Fourth, to counter the feeling held by many of our students that the determiner and tense systems in English are too complex and too unsystematic to learn, we provide instructional material which includes a flow chart (Huckin & Olsen, 1983) and workbook exercises (Frank, 1972). These written materials provide a set of working principles which students can apply later in their speech and in fact, we make it a point to monitor the students' speech for these items (see Figure 1).

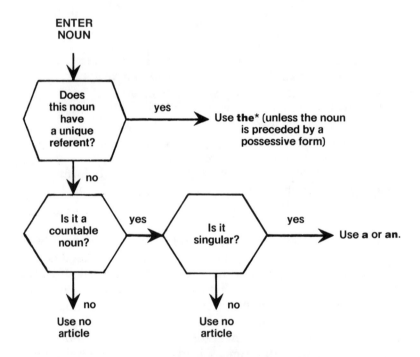

* Or a demonstrative adjective (usually **this** or **these**) under certain special conditions.

Figure 1. Flow chart for choosing the correct article.

Finally, we tell our students that the omission of determiners and inflections can disrupt the natural rhythm of spoken English. To illustrate this, consider the sentence: First we want*ed* to measure *the* crevic*es*. Though native speakers might vary in their intonation of this sentence, they would all give it a flowing rhythm of multiple, unaccented syllables, interrupted by occasional accented ones. By contrast, the nonnative speaker might drop the inflected endings and the article and produce this very measured (i.e., "sing-songy") alternation of strong and weak beats: *"First* we *want* to *meas*ure *crev*ice." Such a rhythm sounds foreign to the native ear. And it results in this case from the omission of the inflected endings and the article.

Rhythm and Contrastive Highlighting

The problem of rhythm has already been touched upon in preceding sections. It can be summarized as follows: Every language of the world has a characteristic speech rhythm which appears to be a product of the syntactic patterning of sentences, phonological constraints, and human physiological constraints. English tends to be a stress-timed language with rhythmic patterns based on a fairly regular recurrence of stressed syllables. Sometimes, as we saw above, the natural order of words lends itself to this kind of regular (but not too regular) recurrence; in cases where this does not happen, native speakers are adept at reducing unstressed syllables, lengthening stressed ones, or inserting pauses so as to make the characteristic rhythm occur. In any case, stress is restricted to those words which are felt to be particularly important in conveying the meaning of the utterance. Hence, speakers (particularly nonnative speakers) must plan ahead and program their sentences before saying them. That is, speakers must anticipate which words are most important so that by applying stress to them and by making various adjustments elsewhere in the sentence (e.g., reducing unstressed syllables or inserting pauses) speakers can produce a native-like speech rhythm.

Languages like French, Japanese, and Hindi, on the other hand, tend to give equal weight to each syllable, making the rhythmic patterns of these languages appear to be more syllable timed. As might be expected, native speakers of syllable-timed languages tend to use this same rhythmic pattern when speaking English. Not only does such a rhythmic pattern sound strange to a native English speaker, but it also fails to give the most important words of the sentence the prominence that native speakers expect to hear. Thus native speakers have to work much harder to determine which words are important, a task which is sometimes impossible in the rapid flow of speech. It has been shown, in fact, that improper speech rhythm is a major contributing factor to incomprehensibility (Adams, 1979).

We address the problem of rhythm in a number of ways, which include providing students with taped and written exercise materials in contractions, linking, sentence stress, and basic intonation patterns (see Morley, 1979). The fact that our students are required for professional reasons to give periodic oral presentations provides us with a natural teaching vehicle.

Using the student's manuscript, we show how to analyze a presentation strategically, that is, how to pick out the most important words of the text and create a rhythmic pattern which puts stress on those words. The following is an excerpt from such a text:

> In many applications, mechanisms are used to perform repetitive operations. During these repetitive operations, there is usually a part of the cycle when the mechanism is under load, an operation called the working stroke, and a part of the cycle when the mechanism is not working but simply returning to repeat the operation, called the return stroke. In order to save energy and time, it is desirable to design the mechanism so that the time required for the return stroke is much shorter than that of the working stroke. For this reason, a drag-link mechanism is usually used in series with another mechanism or device to alter the timing of the return stroke. Practical applications such as drag-link-driven slider-crank mechanisms and drag-link-driven cams can be found in the literature. (Tsai, 1983, p. 688)

Nonnative speakers, reading from such a text, are likely to stress too many content words (i.e., nouns, verbs, adjectives, and adverbs). At the same time they may do one of two things with function words (i.e., prepositions, determiners, pronouns, auxiliaries, and coordinating conjunctions). They may omit them, as we mentioned above, or conversely, they may over-emphasize them. It is precisely such overuse and misuse of stress that produces the foreign-sounding speech rhythms that make speech comprehension difficult. Instead, only those words that are important to the overall meaning of the passage should be given major stress. For example, in this brief text perhaps the two most important terms are *working stroke* and *return stroke.* Since it is the contrast between these two terms that allows the writer to introduce what will eventually become his main topic (drag-link mechanisms), these two terms should be stressed. As this central contrast is elaborated upon, all associated terms and phrases should be emphasized as well.

For example, in the second sentence the subsidiary phrases *under load* and *not working, but simply returning to repeat the operations* are used to define what is meant by *working stroke* and *return stroke* respectively, and so their key words should also be emphasized. Similarly, in the third sentence terms like *time* and *much shorter than* also serve to bring out the central contrast and should be high-lighted. The phrase *for this reason* leading off the fourth sentence serves to connect the preceding general discussion to the more specific discussion about drag-link mechanisms which follows; this phrase should be emphasized also. In short, the coherence of this passage is based on the *working stroke/return stroke* contrast. In an oral presentation of this text the speaker must recognize this contrast and give extra emphasis to the terms and phrases associated with it, without ignoring other important words, such as *repetitive, drag-link mechanism, practical applications, slider-crank,* and *cams.* The speaker should de-emphasize other words, insert pauses, and use other techniques to establish a natural rhythm.

The result would be a text which could be read aloud with lively, emphatic intonation with the important words and phrases all stressed:

> In *many applications, mechanisms* are used to perform *repetitive operations. During* these repetitive operations, there is *usually* a *part* of the *cycle* when the mechanism is under *load,* an operation called the *working* stroke, and a part of the cycle when the mechanism is *not* working but simply *returning* to *repeat* the operation, called the "*return* stroke." In *order* to save *energy* and *time,* it is *desirable* to *design* the mechanism so that the *time required* for the *return* stroke is *much shorter* than that of the *working* stroke. For *this reason,* a *drag-link mechanism* is *usually* used in *series* with *another* mechanism or device to *alter* the *timing* of the *return* stroke. *Practical applications* such as *drag-link*-driven *slider-crank* mechanisms and drag-link-driven *cams* can be found in the *literature.*

These techniques can all be taught explicitly. They do require, however, an ability to divide a text into pause groups, and to evaluate the contributions of the sense group to the major theme or themes of the text. By working with students as informants on their own texts, we call upon their knowledge of the subject matter to help make these judgments. They, in turn, come to understand that the proper use of rhythm is not just a decorative or stylistic touch, but that it actually may be necessary to convey more effectively what they are trying to say.

Observations

Is our approach to these four problems effective? Although it is difficult to measure quantitatively (since the problems are many years in the making and require many months of conscientious effort by our students to correct), all 45 students who have completed our 14-week course have shown some improvement in all four of these problem areas. In some cases progress came quickly and was noticeable even to outsiders; more often, however, it came slowly and was less perceptible.

A summary evaluation of our program by the participants we tutored was conducted at the end of each course. Questionnaires were sent to the participants by the company's program coordinator, Ernest Mazzatenta. The results of these evaluations were relayed to us through reports in which statistically coordinated and analyzed comments about the course (both pro and con) were summarized. These independent reports reveal that the majority of participants preferred private tutorial sessions over any other mode of instruction, and that most actually spent about 3 hours a week working on materials from the tutorial sessions. Finally, these technical professionals rated the practical value of our instruction 7 to 10 on a scale of 1 to 10.

In the long run, however, what counts is our participants' willingness and ability to monitor their own speech patterns. This is where we feel our approach has been most successful. Of the professionals who have completed our course, 80% have continued to come to us for follow-up work.

References

Adams, C. (1979). *English speech rhythm and the foreign learner.* The Hague: Mouton.

Browne, S. (1984). [Sound/spelling materials.] Unpublished materials.

Frank, M. (1972). *Modern English: A practical reference guide.* Englewood Cliffs, NJ: Prentice-Hall.

Hanna, P. R., Hanna, J. S., Hodges, R. E., & Rudorf, E. H., Jr. (1966). *Phoneme-Grapheme correspondence as cues to spelling improvement* (DHEW Publication No. OE-32008). Washington, DC: U.S. Government Printing Office.

Huckin, T. N., & Olsen, L. A. (1983). *English for science and technology: A handbook for nonnative speakers,* New York: McGraw-Hill.

Jassem, W. (1983). *The phonology of modern English,* Warsaw: Panstwowe Wydawnictwo Naukowe.

Longman dictionary of American English: A dictionary for learners of English. (1983). New York: Longman.

Morley, J. (1979). *Improving spoken English.* Ann Arbor: The University of Michigan.

Morley, J. (1985). *Principles, techniques and activities for teaching pronunciation.* Unpublished manuscript.

Morley, J. (in press). *Advanced spoken English.* Ann Arbor: The University of
    Michigan.
Tsai, L. (1983). Design of drag-link mechanisms with minimax transmission angle
    deviation. *Journal of Mechanisms, Transmissions and Automation in Design,*
    105(4), 686-691.

Acknowledgement

An earlier version of this paper is published in the Proceedings of
the 32nd International Technical Communication Conference, Houston, Texas, May, 1985. Copyright at Society for Technical Communication.

Linking and Deletion in Final Consonant Clusters

Mary S. Temperley

University of Illinois at Urbana-Champaign

Editorial Notes

Mary S. Temperley's paper, "Linking and Deletion in Final Consonant Clusters," deals with a rationale for decision making in establishing norms for production of certain English suffixes in contextualized speech. Specifically, Temperley examines word-final consonant clusters, word-initial consonant clusters, and consonant-to-consonant linking across word boundaries in the natural stream of speech.

She suggests that we consider carefully the nature of the modeling we provide for imitation. She cautions against hypercorrect word-in-isolation criteria. Rather, she favors modeling which is characterized by the more naturally occurring deletions and assimilations (especially affrication) that mark correct, informal—but not "bookish"— spoken English.

Whether or not the reader is persuaded to accept her norms, it is Temperley's contention that all students learning to speak and understand English need explicit instruction in linking in order to improve their production. She feels that students need guidance in order to avoid the well-known pitfalls of simply omitting final consonants, overarticulating them, or, in the case of -*ed* suffixes, consistently using a syllabic form.

Temperley provides three carefully constructed tables which display /t/ and /d/ clusters preceding all possible obstruents and nasals. On the tables she indicates with dotted lines those combinations where deletion of final /t/ or /d/ is permissible.

J.M.

Linking and Deletion in Final Consonant Clusters

Many ESL teachers have found themselves in the uncomfortable position of noticing, as they explained the rules for the pronunciation of regular suffixes in English, that their own speech was not providing very convincing examples. For example, they might say *closed books* and realize that the suffix on *closed* was clearly unvoiced. Or, hearing themselves say *closed down*, they might note that the suffix was not there at all. It is similarly awkward when, in continuing their attention to suffixes, they listen to their students read aloud a passage like the following:

> They *called on* an old Aborigine tracker for help . . . his sharp eyes *picked out* the same bootprints he had seen days before . . . They accompanied him as he *followed the* trail . . . The tracker *stopped near* an old, *abandoned cabin* . . .
> (Mellgren & Walker, 1974, p. 131)

Called on and *picked out* are excellent examples, with the suffix clearly pronounced and linked to the next word. *Accompanied him* provides a chance to practice dropping pronominal *h*. *Followed the* is a little more difficult: We do not really want a released stop before the *the*, and we probably do not want *followed de*. Learning to say *-d the* as an affricate is not easy. Should the articulation of this affricate be our target? What about the last two phrases: *stopped near* and *abandoned cabin?* Do we want fully articulated final clusters, or might we settle for no audible ending? What should be our aim?

I spoke recently with a Brazilian teacher of English who had lived for 4 years in the United States some time previously, and studied both in the United States and in her home country. Although her English was excellent, I noticed that she said *askèd him* and *judgèd by*. Furthermore, I was struck by the fact that although I had no doubt about how to correct *askèd him*, I was uncertain about *judgèd by*. In talking with her about these forms later, I told her that we often say *judge' by* with no audible suffix. What are the rules? What generalizations should I give her? Many teachers feel uncertain about norms in this area of English pronunciation—not just about *how* to teach, but *what* to teach. We feel uncertain about words in the stream of speech, about how words are connected, in other words, about *linking*.

Linking: Review of the Literature

Pronunciation texts and manuals treat the subject of linking in various ways. In the 1940's Fries (1945) talked about the "stream of speech." Prator and Robinett's fourth edition of *Manual of American English Pronunciation* (1985) has a good, though short, section on what they call *blending.*

> The blending between the two words of *read it* is as close as that between the two syllables of *reading.* Within a thought group a speaker does not completely interrupt, even for a fraction of a second, the outward flow of breath. (p. 34)

In their chapter on consonant clusters, some further exercises are given to provide practice on linking words, including the use of resyllabification. However, the emphasis is on the importance of pronouncing all the final consonants.

Bowen, in his chapter on English consonant patterns in *Patterns of English Pronunciation* (1975), has many good descriptions and exercises on assimiliation, contraction, and simplification, all of which are aspects of linking. The importance of linking as a basic feature of English pronunciation, like stress and intonation, is implicit rather than explicit in his book.

Mortimer's pronunciation series, *Link-up: A Pronunciation Practice Book* (1977), offers some treatment of linking.

> To pronounce English fluently, it is necessary to link words together as a native speaker of English normally does. Students often fail to do this because they try to pronounce one word at a time or because their own language possesses features which make correct linking in English difficult. (Note on back cover)

However, Mortimer treats only the linking of words ending with a consonant or vowel sound to words beginning with a vowel sound.

In Gilbert's *Clear Speech* (1984), the unit "Linking Words" opens:

> Most university students learn a foreign language mainly through the printed page. This produces a tendency to separate words during speech just as they are separated in print, an unfortunate tendency for people learning English. One of the essential characteristics of English is that the words in a thought group are linked together. If you practice linking words, your speech will become much clearer. (p. 62)

In Gilbert's exercises, the linking of geminate consonant sequences is added to the patterns found in Mortimer: *stop pushing, bad dog,* and so forth.

Although Gimson's *An Introduction to the Pronunciation of English* (1970) has only a short section on liaison (p. 299), he systematically analyzes features of English sounds in context, such as phonetic and phonemic variation, elision, and juncture in several sections of his book (pp. 287-303). Gimson's liaison refers only to the linking of a consonant to a following vowel, and he claims that linking is usual in a final /r/. However, he continues, "it is unusual for a word-final consonant to be carried over as initial in a word beginning with an accented vowel, the identity of the words being retained" (p. 299). It is not clear from this what he thinks happens to the *-d* of *carried over* or the *-n* of *an accented.* But the point is further discussed under juncture (pp. 299-301), where he notes that "junctural oppositions are, in fact, frequently neutralized in connected speech" (p. 301).

Among American ESL texts, Morley's *Improving Spoken English* (1979) comes nearest to recognizing the pervasiveness of linking, relating it to rhythm (lessons 10 & 18), contractions, and sound changes (lessons 12 & 19). Morley offers specific exercises for the practice of linking geminate continuants by "lengthening" and geminate plosives by "holding." She includes a special device to mark those features: *I found some : money* (p.48). She also uses the conventional ligature to indicate the linking, not only of C to V, V to C, and V to V, but of unlike consonants as well: /d/ to /s/ in *The students: sang a sad song*; /l/ to /m/ and, /t/ to /ð/ in *I'll meet you at the bus : stop* (p. 50). Among current texts Morley is unique in using the term linking to include the expanded meaning English pronunciation requires — the attaching of a final consonant to a different consonant.

While Gimson and Morley both recognize that linking takes place even between two unlike consonants, neither author systematically pursues the subject to make explicit its consequences in ESL pronunciation in general, or in the treatment of final consonants and consonant clusters in particular. Closer examination of linking shows its more profound effect on English pronunciation than is usually recognized, and that its neglect leads to misrepresentation and unnatural expectations.

Decision Making in Teaching Pronunciation

English pronunciation teachers must answer some fundamental questions before working to help learners improve their level of comprehension and production. To what features should the teacher draw the students' attention? What can the teacher expect the students to pick up from the incoming stream of speech? What model of connected speech should the teacher use as input?

When I explained to a class that they would be most apt to hear /ǽstɪm/ for *asked him*, one student said, "Now I understand why I don't understand!" Teachers can help improve both comprehension and production by making clear to students what happens to a word in the stream of speech. If the teacher fails to emphasize linking from the beginning of oral work, a powerful tool—a powerful old tool—is neglected in combatting the students' tendency to learn language as individual isolated words with one pronunciation for each word.

In the traditional teaching of French, alternate pronunciations are expected to be made automatically *(Il fait froid* but *Que fait-il? Allez vite* but *Allez-y)*. These alternate forms are studied in context as part of a whole pattern of liaison. Linking is also a fundamental feature in English. Traditional English teaching usually limits its treatment of the morphophonemic effects of linking to the variant shapes of the articles: /ðə/ and /ə/ as opposed to /ðiy/ and /ən/. Linking produces further alterations that we should consider in ESL teaching.

The explicit (though limited) treatment of linking in the texts cited suggests increasing concern with the importance of linking in analysizing and teaching English pronunciation; however, it is still not widely emphasized in the classroom. In questioning an international class of 20 advanced students, I found that only 4 had heard of linking (I described it in various ways) as a feature of spoken English; there was abundant evidence that it was a feature most of them had not acquired. It might be argued that students do not need instruction in linking. Some teachers might say that a learner's transitions between words become more native as fluency develops, or that the lack of these transitions results in nothing worse than a foreign accent. However, we know that a learner can develop fluency without achieving an acceptable level of intelligible pronunciation. Words become linked, but in non-English ways.

If emphasizing linking is important in overcoming the student's tendency to cling to the word as a unit, it is also useful to draw attention to that part of the word which is most notoriously difficult for ESL learners—the end. I have shown elsewhere how linking may be used to emphasize the difference between such troublesome sets as *I, I'd, I've, I'm; interested, interesting;* and *like it, likes it, liked it* (Temperley, 1981). Here I would like to examine linking phenomena more specifically—phenomena conditioned to varying degrees by the following sound. We expect to hear the /d/ of *find* in *find it, find 'im,* or *find out.* Furthermore, it is heard with the following word as *dit, dim, dout,* and a competent speaker of English would expect and produce it as such. In *find some* or *find two,* on the other hand, the presence of the voiced stop is nonsignificant in native speech. Similarly, native speakers do not normally distinguish *planned to* and *plan to.*[1] Comprehensive rules for linking are incomplete, and consequently teachers are uncertain about what to teach.

The lack of attention given to the linking of words is most serious in its effects on learning to pronounce final consonants in general and final-stop consonant clusters in particular. In English language teaching we do not face squarely the problem of choosing clear standards for the pronunciation of the *-ed* suffixes. We have the standard linguistic rules for the pronunciation of regular suffixes. But, as Dickerson (1984) clearly sets forth in "A Learner-Centered Approach to the {Z} and {D} Morphemes," these rules are unsuitable for most ESL learners because they are simply impractical: They expect too much of the learner.

> Nonnative speakers of English may have only marginal aural control over the criteria of siblance and voice and may have little access to phonologically well-formed stems. Thus the inapplicability of the if-statements to ESL learners undermines the whole process of allomorph selection by linguistic rule. (p. 7)

Not only are the rules impractical in ESL teaching, but they are also descriptively inadequate, for they do not always predict regular pronunciations in standard connected speech. Because teachers fail to treat suffixes adequately, students often become proficient in English, attaining a high level in vocabulary and in various aspects of structure, pronunciation, and communicative ability, but lack proficiency at this point where grammar and pronunciation intersect.

Pronunciation of Consonant Sequences

The pronunciation of consonant sequences presents students and teachers alike with problems, and textbooks and manuals provide little systematic help. As a step in remedying this deficiency, I examine the pronunciation of final consonant clusters whose final element is a stop, and the following sound is an obstruent or nasal. Of the approximately 178 final consonant clusters in English, 78 end in a stop. Of these, 67 end in /t/ or /d/. The final /t, d/ clusters and resulting sequences will be examined from three viewpoints: historical, descriptive-prescriptive, and pedagogical. I will explain the development of the difficult sequences, suggest norms for their pronunciation, and propose techniques for helping students produce and understand the normal spoken forms.

In their *Manual,* Prator and Robinett (1985) begin a section on consonant clusters with this statement: "Because the pronunciation of consonant clusters is relatively difficult even for native speakers of English, ways are found to simplify their pronunciation" (p. 153). Some of the various kinds of difficulties include those caused by long and unfamiliar words (e.g., *erythrocytometer*), and by certain stress patterns and sequences of syllable initial consonants (e.g., *communicative, statistics*). But Prator and Robinett are talking about another kind of difficulty, one which English speakers are aware of to some extent: The difficulty produced by sequences of consonants resulting from regular inflections of common words. Probably the most notorious of these are the *-th* words like *sixth, twelfth,* and their plurals. If you think about pronunciation at all, you arc aware that these words are problems, and that in pronouncing them you have to make an effort to overarticulate (or find another way out). There are many more problematic sequences if we are attempting careful speech, singing, or performing on stage. Some examples of such sequences are:

stopped near	abandoned cabin
happened to	changed that
robbed banks	act nicely
well-dressed student	well-dressed man

Or even worse, consider *bribed girls, liked boys, picked pockets,* and *nagged people,* each sequence with three heterogeneous stops.

It is extraordinary that native speakers should find perfectly regular sequences difficult. How can a language have regular consonant patterns that even native speakers find troublesome? The explanation for these difficult sequences is two-part. The first part lies in the historical fact of leveling and loss of suffix vowels in English. This loss produced final consonant clusters that can be regarded as difficult or unnatural.[2] Many of these clusters would have disappeared quite quickly, I suspect, had it not been for the standardization of the spelling system and the spread of literacy. The written forms have become the standard for pronunciation. So we suffer, we find all sorts of ways to avoid them, and we allow some of the written forms to lose their integrity.[3]

The standard written forms prevail, however, when we are consciously thinking about inflections, and above all when we consider acceptable norms or targets for our students' pronunciation. But why, we might ask, did we not keep the syllabic *-ed* suffix after all stops, as we did after /t/ and /d/? It is quite easy to say verb forms, such as *watchèd girls* and *likèd boys,* forms corresponding phonologically to adjectival forms *wretched* and *naked.* We find the second part of the explanation for these difficult forms in looking closely at the articulation of English and its phonotactic probabilities.

In spoken English, word final stops are not normally released independently within a phrase. We say *He sent a letter, He sent the letter, He sent back the letter* with the [t] of *sent* weakly released into the *a*, combined with the [ð] of *the*, or incomplete, with no audible release before another stop (Gimson, 1970). Although sequences of two consonants, even two stops, are common in English as in *actor* or *flag pole*, the first is checked and not normally released. Laying aside semantic considerations, we can say that the perception of the final stop is determined in part by the anticipatory shape and length of the preceding stop, and in part by the assimilatory effects of the two consonants. We can say *first^h grade* or *robbed^ɔ banks*, but it sounds somewhat artificial. Instead, the stop is usually released into the following vowel or continuant. If the stop is preceded by another stop (not released at all, even when the first stop is pronounced where we have the first two stages of closure and hold). A stop preceded by another stop cannot be released easily without breaking the flow of the English phrase. But these facts only make the sequences of obstruent-stop-obstruent seem more unnatural. Why did they become the standard form? Because the difficult sequences are relatively rare.

Word-Final Obstruent-Stop Clusters

The various sequences in which final cluster obstruent + /t, d/ may occur can be seen in Table 1. In the first group the final consonant is easily released into the following vowel, semivowel, /h/, or liquid. In the second group the point of articulation of the final consonant is close to or identical with that of the following initial consonant. This makes the apparent production of three stops relatively manageable. I say apparent because preceding an alveolar stop the presence of a final post-obstruent /t/ or /d/ is devoid of practical significance. But as native speakers we are unaware of this; we do not think about whether the final stop is there or not. It is only in the third group that the word-final stop must be independently released. I suggest that the obstruent-stop clusters are retained in English pronunciation because they can be accommodated in the ways shown in 1. and 2. of Table 1. Apart from the (really hopeless) cases of the -*th* words mentioned above, the serious pronunciation problems for native speakers occur only when an obstruent-stop cluster is followed by a word beginning with a heterogeneous obstruent or nasal. The necessity for pronouncing these nonhomorganic sequences does not arise very often; when it does, we may make a special effort to release the stop within the phrase, or more

Table 1. Sequences Formed with Word-Final Obstruent-Stop Clusters

The word-final consonant —

1. passed over	/-st V-/	⎫
breathed weakly	/-ɤd w-/	⎪ is released into the following
grabbed you	/-bd y-/	⎬ vowel, semivowel or /h/.
gift horse	/-ft h-/	⎭
act rationally	/-kt r-/	⎫ is released into the following
begged lawyers	/-gd l-/	⎭ liquid.
2. chopped things	/-pt θ-/	⎫
list that	/-st ɤ-/	⎪
pushed some	/-št s-/	⎬ forms an affricate with the
watched zebras	/-čt z-/	⎭ following /C/.
rubbed shoes	/-bd š-/	
hugged no one	/-gd n-/	
accept two	/-pt t-/	and the following /C/ are
judged deeds	/-ǰd d-/	homorganic.
stacked change	/-kt č-/	The presence of the final /C/
squeezed juice	/-zd ǰ-/	is moot.
3. laughed politely	/-ft p-/	⎫
loathed coke	/-ɤd k-/	⎪
kissed babies	/-st b-/	⎪
looked good	/-kt g-/	⎬ must be articulated inde-
last Friday	/-st f-/	pendently of the following
changed vans	/-ǰd v-/	/C/, if at all.
amazed me	/-zd m-/	⎭

often, we approximate the sound.

What do we do with word-final /t, d/ in consonant sequences? Dictionary citation forms and the standard rules for the pronunciation of suffixes are incomplete in providing useful targets for pronunciation. Because they fail to provide a realistic account of native speech, standard rules of pronunciation are unsuitable for ESL learners (Dickerson, 1984) and inadequate for ESL teaching. There are many situations where we do not produce or expect to hear the fully articulated, word-in-isolation forms with the clearly voiceless or voiced released stops that the standard rules and dictionaries specify. These are cases where the word-final stop may be devoiced, linked to the following consonant, both of these, or deleted entirely.

Linking and Deletion in Final /t, d/ Clusters

Assuming that there is a range in native speech which can reasonably be used as a target in ESL teaching, at one extreme are isolated-word or platform style pronunciations, at the other are rapid forms labeled "uneducated," "sloppy," "unintelligible," or some red-flagged area of disrepute which diverts the hearer's attention from message to code. To make it easier to deal with this large amount of data, I present Tables 2, 3, and 4 of word-final /t, d/ consonant clusters with following consonants. I have not included sequences of final /t, d/ after a vowel regardless of their morphological status, nor final /t, d/ clusters before a vowel or pause. Nor have I included examples of /t, d/ clusters before /w, y, h, r, l/. I assume that the omission of a single final stop consonant is unacceptable, and I assume a norm for the clusters before a vowel which has some audible manifestation of the final consonant. The full form of even the worst clusters is more easily linked to these sounds than to obstruents and nasals, and according to deletion studies is more commonly preserved (Guy, 1980). Thus, we are left with the consideration of possible pronunciations of final /t, d/ clusters before obstruents and nasals. On the tables I have included both inflected and monomorphemic forms where they exist.[4]

Table 2. Linking and Deletion in Final Consonant Clusters

Charts of consonant sequences in phrases consisting of words with a final /t/ or /d/ cluster followed by words with initial obstruents or nasals

All final /-t, -d/ two-consonant clusters are included, with the exception of the rare /-θt/ (as in *unearthed* or [Brit.] *bathed*) and /-ẓd/ (*rouged, garaged*). For clusters with antepenultimate consonants, see note 4. Where they occur, both monomorphemic and bimorphemic examples of a cluster are shown, by two rows of phrases in a box. The bimorphemic forms for /-rt, -lt, -nt/ are, of course, irregular forms; *hurt* is a unique bimorphemic form.

	f-	v-	θ-	ð-	s-, z-	š-	n-	m-
-rt	heart failure / (hurt few	short version / hurt Vera,	start things / etc.)	sort those	shirt sleeve	short shrift	sort nails	smart money
-rd	hard feelings / bored friends	toward vice / steered vans	hoard things / peered thru	afford those / adored that	yard sale / feared Zeus	herd sheep / neared shore	bird nest / feared no one	hard man / bored many
-lt	wilt flowers / felt funny	halt vice / spelt victory	pelt things / felt things	bolt those / dealt them	gilt spoon / dealt some	felt shoes / felt sure	halt now / felt no pain	salt marsh / spoilt me
-ld	old friends / filed folders	cold venison / filled vases	wild thought / filled things	hold those / called there	mild spring / filled zoos	old shoes / called sharply	old nanny / killed no one	bold man / pulled many
-nt	want food / sent families	count voices / sent volumes	want things / meant things	want those / sent them	blunt scissors / spent some	want shampoo / sent sugar	blunt knife / spent none	Aunt Mary / spent money

	p-	b-	t-	d-	č-	ǯ-	k-	g-
-rt	start playing / (hurt people	start back / hurt both,	short time / etc.)	art deco	short change	start jogging	smart cat	art gallery
-rd	sword play / bored people	toward Boston / gored bulls	hard times / feared tigers	card dealer / barred drunks	word choice / toured China	toward goals / poured gin	hard coal / feared cats	word game / deployed guns
-lt	salt pork / felt pleased	salt box / spoilt boxes	melt tar / felt terrible	bolt doors / knelt down	melt chocolate / felt chilly	gilt jewelry / dealt justice	felt covers / dealt kindly	melt gold / felt good
-ld	cold potatoes / filed past	hold back / spilled beer	cold turkey / filled tables	mild disease / rolled dough	old church / spilled chips	old joke / piled junk	wild caper / called kitty	hold gallons / filled glasses
-nt	count pennies / sent papers	want business / bent back	count tips / sent tons	Aunt Di / meant death	count charge / lent charm	want justice / sent jam	want cash / spent cash	pint glass / burnt gas

Table 3.

	f-	v-	θ-	ɣ-	s-, z-	š--	n-	m-
-ft	lift fingers laughed freely	gift volumes coughed violently	lift things sloughed things off	lift that muffed that	soft soap coughed silently	left shoe laughed shamelessly	left nostril coughed nervously	soft money laughed merrily
-vd	loved phoning	moved vaguely	loved thinking	moved those	loved zoos	behaved shamefully	saved nothing	moved mountains
-ɤd	breathed freely	loathed vacations	loathed theory	soothed them	breathed silently	loathed shaving	breathed noisily	loathed money
-st	last Friday passed finals	last violin missed veins	first things passed things	just then guessed that	last summer missed some	just shows tossed shoes	best night missed none	last month fussed most
-št	finished phoning	finished voting	wished things	washed those	washed socks	finished shopping	finished knitting	wished most
-zd	amazed friends	closed veins	used things	used that	used soap	closed shops	used knives	amazed me
-md	seemed fine	seemed vexed	seemed thin	timed that	framed sets	seemed sure	aimed near	seemed mad
-ŋd	longed for	banged vans	banged things	belonged there	belonged somewhere	wronged Shirley	belonged nowhere	wronged many
-nd	round face owned fields	sound voice owned vans	round things canned things	send those planned this	find some owned six	find shoes planned shows	spend none banned nets	find money banned movies
°-pt	accept fines	accept votes	accept things	adapt those	adopt signs	inept shot	inept note	accept money
-bd	robbed Fred	robbed Vicky	nabbed things	nabbed that	grabbed some	robbed shops	ebbed nearly	grabbed men
°-kt	expect fun looked funny	act violent liked violins	expect things looked thin	exact that worked there	act silly liked silk	concoct shows licked sugar	act nice lacked nerve	act mad worked madly
-gd	lugged folders	lugged victims	rigged things	rigged that	begged silently	begged shoes	bugged no one	egged me on
-čt	reached Frisco	matched viols	clutched things	reached there	matched slips	watched shows	matched nothing	watched many
-jd	judged fairly	changed vans	changed things	urged that	changed sides	changed shoes	changed nothing	changed much

Table 4.

	p-	b-	t-	d-	č-	ǰ-	k-	g-
-ft	lift pounds / laughed politely	lift bales / laughed bitterly	left turn / coughed terribly	soft dough / laughed during it	left cheek / laughed cheerfully	left jaw / sniffed jam	lift cases / laughed carelessly	lift guns / laughed gaily
-vd	behaved poorly	loved books	moved tables	moved dirt	moved chairs	behaved justly	loved coffee	loved gum
-ᶞd	bathed puppies	bathed babies	breathed twice	loathed dishes	bathed chimps	loathed juice	loathed coke	loathed gum
-st	last part / missed parties	last bastion / kissed babies	last time / passed twice	last dime / passed drivers	last chance / missed choosing	best job / passed judgment	best kind / guessed quickly	just great / passed goal
-št	washed plates	finished batting	wished to	pushed down	finished chapters	finished judging	pushed carefully	finished going
-zd	pleased people	used both	closed twice	closed doors	raised chicks	squeezed juice	used commas	closed gaps
-md	framed pictures	seemed best	timed tests	seemed dim	seemed changed	seemed jealous	aimed carefully	consumed grapes
-ŋd	wronged people	ringed birds	ringed trees	banged doors	banged chairs	ringed jars	belonged closer	banged gongs
-nd	send parcels / owned places	spend billions / owned barns	send trainers / rained torrents	mind daddy / planned dinners	mind choosing / owned chairs	grand jury / planned jaunts	find cause / planned courses	send girls / owned galleries
°-pt	accept payment / sipped pernod	except bacon / helped buy	accept tokens / stopped trying	except dinner / slipped disc	inept choice / helped choose	inept judgment / stopped jumping	accept calls / stopped calling	adopt girls / helped get
-bd	robbed people	rubbed brasses	robbed trains	robbed dozens	robbed churches	bribed juries	grabbed cash	grabbed gobs
°-kt	act properly / kicked people	elect both / looked bad	duct tape / lacked time	expect donors / looked down	act cheery / liked cheese	act jolly / looked jealous	act quickly / baked cookies	expect gold / looked good
-gd	hugged people	begged bread	flagged trains	hugged dolls	hugged children	rigged juries	drugged kids	bagged game
-čt	searched passengers	searched bags	watched telly	reached down	reached China	switched jackets	reached campus	watched glands
-ǰd	changed places	charged batteries	changed trains	judged dozens	arranged chairs	changed jobs	changed courses	enlarged glands

Deletion

I pose the basic questions: (a) Are final stops deletable, and if so where; and if not (b) how are the words linked?

Defining deletion.

We must agree on what we mean by keeping and deleting a stop (e.g., word final /t, d/). The stop may be represented by the full three-stage articulation (closure, hold, release) or by only the first two stages with the release coming in the articulation of the following consonant. There may be glottal reinforcement of a cluster-ending voiceless stop and vowel lengthening before a voiced stop cluster (Gimson, 1970, pp. 150-159). We might want to consider other articulatory features, but for now let us say that by "keeping a stop," we mean that we produce an articulation which audibly distinguishes the phrase, from the phrase with no stop.

By "deleting" we mean that we produce a phrase where the stop has no clear manifestation. If we consider how these words are to be linked, we find various options or possibilities for target pronunciations. We could choose as our goal a pronunciation in which all final stops are kept with a full, three-stage articulation, as in $last^h$ time or $supposed^\circ$ to. I think most of us would regard this as unrealistic, but I do not mean to rule it out. Some teachers might advocate this target for an early stage of pronunciation instruction. At the other extreme, we could decide that in these sequences the final stop is deletable. But this is immediately seen to be too sweeping if we look at the phrases on Table 2 where we would, I feel sure, agree on the need for keeping the stop in most, if not all, of the cases; *part score* is to be distinguished from *par score, halt vice* from *hall vice,* and so forth. If this is so, then it follows that in linking the words on the three tables, the final consonant is differentially deletable—sometimes dropped and sometimes not. For purposes of pursuing the argument, I suggest a set of personal norms (not data from an empirical study) that are proposed in the belief that an ESL teacher must have standards of acceptability similar to these, whether consciously or unconsciously.

Table 2.

In clusters with /r/ and /l/, loss of the final stop is not my norm. The final stop is not released; a released stop sounds abnormal here. Note the difference between the /t/ and /d/ clusters: loss of /t/ is impossible for me, as is loss of /d/ after /r/. *Wor' processor, har' coal* are unacceptable, but *col' potatoes, mil' curry* might be admitted. Dropping the /d/ after /l/ in monomorphemic words is more acceptable than doing it in inflected forms. *I lik col' potatoes* is better than *Yesterday I peel' potatoes.*

These preferences correspond to the generally agreed upon principle that deletion occurs only when there is voicing agreement between the consonants in a cluster (Wolfram & Fasold, 1974, p. 131). In addition, they concur with Guy's findings (1980) that preceding /r/ promotes /t, d/ retention more than /l/ (the effect of /r/ is like that of a vowel), and that suffixed forms are less likely to lose /t, d/ than monomorphemic forms. I have included the /nt/ clusters with /r/ and /l/; the stop is to be preserved here also. This does not mean that the linking of the final /t/ with a following /š/ will sound the same as /č/; *meant shoes* will still be different from *men choose*. *Plant twice* will also be different from *plan twice*. I do not advocate deletion of final /t/ and /d/ as target pronunciations for the phrases on this table.

Tables 3 and 4.

Now we consider the final clusters on Table 3, those beginning with fricatives, nasals, and stops (excluding /nt/). I have indicated the norms I suggest by a dotted line. Before sibilants and /n/, the final stop can be lost. Similarly, on Table 4 my norm requires no final alveolar stop—final /t, d/—before an initial alveolar stop or affricate. Note that in these sequences, the presence of the final /t, d/ is moot. We can pronounce a final stop without releasing it by prolonging the silence to make it geminate: *coughed̲ terribly, seemed̲ dim,* as opposed to *cough' terribly, seem'dim*. But this difference is devoid of practical significance.

The other areas where my table indicates no final stop are somewhat different: /nd/ and two-stop clusters before all other stops. These are real cases of deletion. One can distinguish between *send parcels* and *sen' parcels,* but the only way that the presence of the final stop can be indicated is by its release, although it is not the normal pattern of articulation (cf. Gimson, 1970, p. 298). An abnormal pattern of articulation, a released stop, will be required to keep the /t/ and /d/ preceding the stops in the upper half of the first two and last columns before /p/, /b/, /k/, and /g/ (e.g., *behaved̲ poorly; pushed̲ carefully,* etc.). The relative infrequency of these sequences may influence my decision to keep the word-final stop. Perhaps a speaker is prepared to make more effort for a rare sequence, just as for a rare word. The loss of the stop between the homorganic consonants seems better than between nonhomorganic ones: Omitting the /d/ in *He frame' pictures* is better than in *He wrong' people; He bang' gongs* is better than *He guess' quickly*. The pattern of a prolonged consonant replacing a consonant sandwich is familiar. Morphology also makes a difference: Deletion in *They ate can' meat* is better than in *He ban' movies.* But let me summarize my position before going on to discuss the further effects of linking. Final alveolar stops are deleted in fricative, stop, affricate, and voiced nasal clusters before alveolar obstruents and nasals, and in /-nd/ and stop and affricate clusters before all other stops as well.[5]

Linking

This brings us to the second question: If the final consonant is not deleted, how is it linked to the following initial consonant? One set of patterns provides ways of avoiding independent release of the word-final stop, and another set ways of minimizing it.

Avoiding independent release of the word-final stop.

Gemination and affricatization remove the possibility of releasing the stop. *Gemination,* or lengthening of the holding stage, may occur where the final /t, d/ are followed by an alveolar stop or affricate (as in column 3-6 in the lower half of Table 2): *short time, bolt doors, old church, piled junk. Affricate articulation* can link a final alveolar stop to a following initial fricative (columns 3-6, Table 2; and columns 3-4, Table 3): *start things, hold those, mild spring, sent sugar, loved thinking, washed those.*

Minimizing the release of the word-final stop.

In the difficult cases where my formulation requires a release of the word-final, phrase-medial stop, two other patterns of articulation mitigate its effect: devoicing and resyllabification. Pronunciation texts (as well as our own ears) tell us that if a final voiced stop is retained, it is devoiced (partially or wholly) before a voiceless sound. But if one listens carefully or actually tries to maintain voicing of a stop between two voiced consonants, one realizes that voicing is very weak or even absent here also: *laze[d] by the pool, hugge[d] Vera, change[d] bats, frame[d] those.* Full voicing throughout these sequences sounds very odd. Spectrograms show that voicing often disappears in this position. The articulation is still lenis, but weakening of the voicing produces a still weaker release.

The other means of minimizing the stop-release (resyllabification) is discussed briefly in Prator and Robinett (1985), Gilbert (1984, p. 63), and Morley (1979, p. 50). These authors recognize the linkage of the final C to a following initial V and use a hyphen, readjusted spacing, or both to show the revised syllable boundary: *charge-dout, sai dit, pi-cki-tup.* However, they do not go far enough in noting the overriding effects of linking; within the phonological phrase, the final consonant is closely linked to the following word, whatever the initial sound of that word. That is, we say not only *laze-din* but *laze-dby; frame-dit* but *frame-dthose; hugge-dim* but *hugge-dVera.* We can retain pronunciation with three or more obstruents, even three or more stops. We can say *She hugged Bob,* articulating all three stops with only a slight interruption in the flow of the phonological phrase. But the interruption is after the first stop, not after the second where the orthographic space is. An acceptable production requires the rapid articulation of the second stop and the linking of it to the third: *She hugge-dBob,* not *She hugged² Bob.* Notice that these two minimizing features of devoicing (of /d/) and resyllabification are present in the cases where the final stop is not deleted, including those sequences inside the dotted lines on the charts (if my deletion forms are rejected as acceptable target pronunciations).

Techniques for Teaching Linking

I do not expect my targets to be readily accepted, rather I propose them as a means of accelerating the discussion of linking. In spite of the uncertain state of the norms, we can see the consequences of linking and deletion in ESL teaching. Students are not likely to learn an acceptable pronunciation of English by conscientiously stringing together separately articulated words.

In several texts, as noted in our review of the literature, we find discussions and exercises devoted to some aspects of linking, in addition to various methods for presenting the subject graphically. My first suggestion is to recommend a more pervasive, comprehensive, and explicit use of linked forms. This means the use of phrases, and more consistent and systematic emphasis on the pronunciation of contextualized forms *from the beginning of English instruction.* Even the earliest exercises in English sounds, given in the form of lists of separate words, can be framed in short phrases: noun phrases or verb/object phrases. Emphasis on linking draws needed attention to the end of words, in addition to the beginning. Specifically, exercises with linked forms can help overcome students' tendencies to use glottal stops before initial vowels and to pronounce initial unstressed *h.*

More emphasis also can be placed on gemination, following Morley's (1979) and Gilbert's (1984) models. In addition, affricates, particularly final stops with initial *th* sounds, such as *use-dthings, planne-dthis, looke-dthin,* and *change-dthings,* can be stressed. These are similar to the exercises proposed by both Prator and Robinett (1972, pp. 155-156) and Bowen (1975, p. 237). The need for systematic work with resyllabification can be seen all too clearly in students' response to "not pronouncing the spaces" between words. Asking students to say *sen-dit,* I sometimes have as a response *sendit it.* Although conceptualization of such linking can be difficult for some students, I urge its use in all cases. We must provide more practice and emphasis on the difficult initial clusters which result from the restructuring of syllables in such cases as *col-dbeer, fas-tgirls, cooke-tfish, behave-dbadly,* and *change-dvans,* where we expect the stop to be retained.

Finally, as in Dickerson (1984), I emphasize the importance of concentrating on the presence of the final stop in our obstruent-stop sequences, rather than on the nature of its voicing. In the sequences with liquids on Table 2, the contrast between /t/ and /d/ is maintained, but it is more properly described as a contrast in tension between fortis and lenis, rather than in actual voicing. As we move to the obstruent clusters, however, where the choice between the two stops is said to be automatic, this opposition is neutralized; the difference between the final alveolars of *accept things* and *nabbed things* or *lift that* and *move those* is not significant. The significant contrast between the two stops lessens as the sequence becomes more consonantal and culminates in my formulation with the disappearance of the stop altogether between stops.

Teaching Deletion?

This brings us back to deletion and to the practical consequences of recognizing it as normal and differentially encouraging it. Most of us believe we can improve (dare I say teach?) pronunciation. But does it make sense to speak of teaching deletion? We do attempt some training in deletion of the initial *h* in unstressed pronouns or deletions leading to the common contractions. But the rules for those are relatively simple compared to the kind of formulation I have presented.

I do not suggest giving my proposed norms directly to any but the most advanced students or teacher-trainees. Both active and passive techniques are suggested for promoting the production of these forms. Actively, one can call attention to acceptable cases of deletion and provide practice in producing forms showing the most common patterns, such as, *used to, supposed to, accustomed to; closed Tuesday, moved down, arrived Sunday; seemed tired, planned carefully, changed planes.* Further, one can offer exercises in contrasting forms: *he kep-tasking, she kep-tlistening,* but *they kept driving; he arrive-dlast week, she arrive-dyesterday,* but *the children arrived Tuesday; she move-daway, he move-d back,* but *they moved down; she owne-dland, he owne-dhouses,* but *they owned nothing.* At this level, some part of a rule can also be given; for example, /-t, -d/, *-ed* are deletable after *p, k, b, g, ch* before *t-* (not *th-*), *d-, ch-, j-; -d* and *-ed* are similarly deletable after *n.* Certain consonants can be marked for deletion in preparation for reading aloud.

On a passive level, one can simply ignore (perhaps inwardly noting) acceptably deleted forms whatever their origin, and emphasize the production of final consonants only in sequences where one's rules require them. I assume a position here similar to the one I take for final -s clusters: If students can produce the full, undeleted forms without undue difficulty, I leave it at that (Temperley, 1983). If they are having difficulty, practice with some deletion forms may help.

> He wrapped some and sol-dsome.
> She found some and lost some.
> He hear-dsome and tol-dsome.
> She caught some and tossed some.

Along with giving students practice in producing and listening to linked forms, teachers may want a way of representing linking graphically. Conventional orthography does not help us to de-emphasize the word—quite the contrary. However, students have to learn not to depend on the spaces between words as unfailing guides to pronunciation. If a phonemic transcription is used, spaces can be removed within the phrase, as in (a), or used to indicate that a following syllable is accented (b). Without using a special alphabet one can use the conventional linking symbol as in (c), or hyphens and adjusted spacing as in (d).

> (a) /šiyəràyvdléyt | nkèptókıŋ/
> (b) /šiyə rayv-dleyt | n kɛp tɔkıŋ/
> (c) She‿arrived‿late ‿and‿kept‿talking.
> (d) She arrive-dlate 'n' kep' talking.

Final Notes

The current trends in English language teaching place little emphasis on pronunciation and its grammatical consequences. This may be due in part to the fact that the conventionally stated form of the English inflectional system requires intrinsically difficult and unnatural articulations. The result is that even pronunciation teachers are uncertain about what to teach. Furthermore, the unprecedented number of English learners worldwide is putting great pressure on the inflectional system; it is continually being weakened and may well disappear. Perhaps English teachers should just flow with this tide. However, if they chose not to, they must study native speakers' patterns of linking and deletion, and answer the questions of acceptability that they raise.

References

Bowen, J. D. (1975). *Patterns of English pronunciation.* Rowley, MA: Newbury House.

Dickerson, W. (1984, March). *A learner-centered approach to the {Z} {D} morphemes.* Paper presented at the 18th Annual TESOL Convention, Houston.

Fries, C. C. (1945). *Teaching and learning English as a foreign language.* Ann Arbor: The University of Michigan.

Gilbert, J. B. (1984). *Clear speech: Pronunciation and listening comprehension in American English.* Cambridge: Cambridge University.

Gimson, A. C. (1970). *An introduction to the pronunciation of English (2nd ed.).* London: Edward Arnold.

Greenberg, J. H. (n.d.). Unpublished notebooks.

Guy, G. R. (1980). Variation in the group and the individual: The case of final stop deletion. In W. Labov (Ed.), *Locating language in time and space* (pp. 1-36). New York: Academic Press.

Mellgren, L, & Walker, M. (1974). *New horizons in English* (Book 5). Reading, MA: Addison-Wesley.

Morley, J. (1979). *Improving spoken English.* Ann Arbor: The University of Michigan.

Mortimer, C. (1977). *Link-up: A pronunciation practice book.* Cambridge: Cambridge University.

Prator, C. H., Jr., & Robinett, B. W. (1985). *Manual of American English pronunciation (4th ed.).* New York: Holt, Rinehart & Winston.

Temperley, M. S. (1981). The stream of speech and what to do about it. In J. Haskell & R. Orem (Eds.), *Selected papers from the ninth Illinois TESOL BE annual convention first midwest TESOL conference* (pp. 17-24). Champaign, IL.

Temperley, M. S. (1983). The articulatory target for final -s clusters. *TESOL Quarterly, 17*(3), 421-436

Wolfram, W, & Fasold, R. (1974). *The study of social dialects in American English.* Englewood Cliffs, NJ: Prentice-Hall.

Wolfram, W. & Johnson, R. (1982). *Phonological analysis.* Washington, DC: Center for Applied Linguistics

Footnotes

[1]See Guy (1980) for an analysis of the various factors promoting /-t, -d/ deletion.

[2]This follows from the formulation that the most natural syllable structure is CV and that voiceless obstruents are more natural in final position than voiced. Wolfram and Johnson's (1982) discussion of naturalness concludes with an excellent description of what happened to English suffixation, and of the processes we are dealing with here.

> The natural by-product of a particular process may be some unnatural syllables or sequences. The natural process of vowel reduction, carried to its extreme, might result in removing the vowel altogether, which in turn, might have the effect of bringing two consonants together. For example, the loss of a vowel in the unstressed syllables of *police* and *baloney* might be naturally motivated, but would also result in an initial consonant cluster ([plis], [bloni]). This introduces a less natural sequence, and the need for another process to begin to bring the sequence back toward the ideal CV pattern. This sort of adjustment and readjustment, in combination with the effects of language contact, must certainly be part of the reason for constant change in all phonological systems. (p.163)

English seems to be one of only two languages in Greenberg's survey (n.d) that uses the full range of voiced obstruent final clusters:

	fricative	stop
fricative & affricative	loves, loathes (3)	loved, loathed, closed, rouged, judged (8)
stop	ebbs, Ed's, eggs (4)	ebbed, egged (6)

(Note: Clusters occur in (?) other language.) The other language with all four sets is Georgian.

³The most obvious illustration can be seen in constructions such as *mash potatoes* and *ice coffee*, where an original past participle form, when preposed, loses its suffix even in writing. Many of these are so common as to be almost unnoticeable, our common noun-noun construction often conveniently supplying a reinterpretation of the phrase. But once in a while one does stand out: *can vegetables* on a sign in a grocery store; *close Monday* outside a restaurant; *mix berry* and *toss green salad* on labels in a cafeteria.

⁴Many of these two-consonant final clusters may be preceded by a third consonant: a liquid or nasal. Final /-st/ may also be preceded by the stops /p, t, k, d/ (*lapsed, against, next, midst;*/ læpst, agɛnst, nɛkst, mɪdst;/) and /-zd/ by /d/ (*dazed*). In these clusters the presence of the antepenultimate consonant does not affect my formulations. The clusters marked °, however, may be preceded by /s/, as in *risked, grasped* /rɪskt, græspt/. Here the situation is more complicated. The form *asked*, no doubt because of its frequency, seems to be a special case: There is a rule for some standard dialects, *asked* /æst/, which makes /æst/ the full or canonical form. If this rule is applied, then *asked* is placed in the /-st/ boxes along with *last* and *passed*, and the final /t/ deleted accordingly. But these rules do not apply to other /-s+stop+stop/ forms: *risked* does not automatically become /rɪst/, nor *grasped* /græst/. There is variation in the pronunciation of these forms, but neither deletion form (risked ——› /rɪst/ or rɪsk/) seems normal. My rules are thus not to be taken to apply to the /-s ≠ stop ≠ stop/final clusters.

I omit clusters ending with the other stops and affricates (/p, b, k, g, č, ǰ/) because these clusters are formed for the most part with liquids and nasals as the first element: They are easy clusters. Furthermore, clusters ending with these stops and affricates are monomorphemic: The final consonant never represents a suffix. For a discussion of pronunciation problems arising with -*s* suffixes added to /-s+stop/ stems, see Temperley (1983).

⁵This formulation is similar to but less inclusive than Wolfram and Fasold's: "In Standard English, the final member of the cluster may be absent if the following word begins with a consonant, so that *bes' kind, col' cuts*, and *wes' side* are common and acceptable in spoken Standard English." (1974, p. 131)

Phonetics and the Teaching of Pronunciation: A Systemic Description of English Phonology

J. C. Catford

The University of Michigan

Editorial Notes

Observing that before one can teach anything, it is necessary to know what one is to teach, J. C. Catford begins "Phonetics and the Teaching of Pronunciation" with a description of the sound system of English. His presentation of English phonology is a *systemic* one that derives from the *systemic linguistics* associated with the British linguist M. A. K. Halliday. This system is formulated in a four-rank hierarchy of units, with every unit at one rank consisting of one or more units of the rank below it. He emphasizes the point that for the teaching of pronunciation it is important to think of English phonology as a series, a hierarchy of units of different kinds, not merely as a collection of sound segments whose pronunciation must be learned so that they can be strung together with stresses and intonations superimposed on them. The four units are: (a) *tone group*, (b) *foot*, (c) *syllable*, and (d) *phoneme*.

Catford then turns to a discussion of three distinct types of process in pronunciation instruction: selection, arrangement, and presentation of materials to be taught. In the section on selection Catford suggests that two principles—*frequency of occurrence* and *functional load*—be followed in selecting particular sounds for teaching. In Catford's terms frequency of occurrence is the number of times a sound occurs per thousand words in text. (Voiced *th* is the highest frequency sound in English.) Functional load refers to the number of words in the lexicon in which the sound occurs, or in the case of a contrast, the number of pairs of words that it serves to keep distinct. (/i/ɪ/ has a high functional load in English, while /u/ʊ/ has a low functional load.)

In the section on arrangement Catford suggests the following sequencing of pronunciation points for instruction: (a) basic rhythm and intonation patterns; (b) syllable openings and closings, specifically syllable-initial consonants, syllable-final consonants, and consonant clusters; (c) open transition between consonants, usually regarded as a short unstressed vowel as illustrated by the first word of these pairs: *terrain/train, parade/prayed, scallop/scalp, chorus/course;* and (4) vowels and diphthongs (i.e., the syllabic nuclei).

Finally, Catford focuses on presentation and outlines five principles: (a) precise descriptions; (b) concentration on teaching basics, not symptoms; (c) introspection and silent practice; (d) utilization of all sounds known to the student, that is, capitalizing on the articula-

tion possibilities available to students from their own languages; and
(e) imitation and slowed-down speech. The material presented in
these five sections of presentation contains a wealth of examples and
a number of carefully described teaching techniques.

Catford concludes with the comment that using phonetics in teaching pronunciation means to many only a narrow concept of using
phonetic transcription. In fact, according to Catford, it really means
using *applied phonetics* — the information and the skills that the careful study of phonetics can provide.

J. M.

Phonetics and the Teaching of Pronunciation:
A Systemic Description of English Phonology

Before one can teach anything it is necessary to know what one is going to teach! So I begin with a short survey of English pronunciation.

There are various ways of describing the sound system of English. One description which I find particularly useful for the organization of pronunciation teaching is a *systemic* description of English phonology derived from the *systemic linguistics* associated with M. A. K. Halliday.

In this description, the sound system of English is regarded as a hierarchy of units at four ranks. It moves from the largest or most inclusive unit, the intonation contour or *tone group,* to the rhythmic unit, or *foot;* to the *syllable;* and finally to the smallest unit, the phonemic unit or *phoneme.* Every unit at one rank consists of one or more units of the rank below it. That is, every tone group consists of one or more foot, every foot of one or more syllable, every syllable of one or more phoneme.

The following is an example of an English sentence with the various ranks in the phonological hierarchy indicated:

The book we read was interesting.

Chart 1

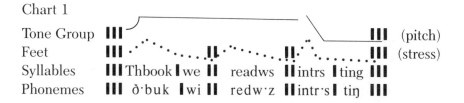

Tone Group	**III**				**III** (pitch)
Feet	**III**	**II**	**II**		**III** (stress)
Syllables	**III** Thbook **I** we **II**	readws	**II** intrs **I** ting	**III**	
Phonemes	**III** ðˑbuk **I** wi **II**	redwˑz	**II** intrˑs **I** tiŋ	**III**	

As this simplified example indicates, tone group consists of one continuous intonation contour with a single dynamic (falling) tone. Each foot consists of a single stress impulse, rising quickly to a peak near the beginning of the foot and then falling off more slowly, as indicated by the dotted line representing the quickly rising then falling stress pulse. The syllables are written with some vowels omitted to indicate that *th, ws,* and *trs* do not form syllables in themselves. They are better regarded as pseudosyllables tacked onto real syllables and containing *open transitions*. The last rank consists of phonemes and of open transitions between consonants which are represented by [ˑ] (see Catford, 1966, 1985, for further information).

The above account of the phonological hierarchy of English emphasizes an essential point in pronunciation teaching. English phonology is not merely a collection of phonemes whose pronunciation has to be learned and later strung together with superimposed stresses and intonations, but rather a *hierarchy* of units of different kinds, each with its own learning problems.

Selection, Arrangement, and Presentation

Teaching pronunciation involves at least three distinct types of process: selection, arrangement, and presentation of material.

Selection

The first of these processes, selection, is necessary because clearly one cannot teach a whole language in any particular course. This is generally appreciated with respect to vocabulary and grammar, but it is often forgotten in pronunciation teaching. The result may be either a half-hearted attempt to teach every feature of pronunciation, or no attempt is made at all. Pronunciation is regarded as too complex and vast an area.

However, it is perfectly possible to make a deliberate selection of items to be taught. The *principle of frequency* often used in vocabulary selection can also be applied to pronunciation. In the initial stages one might restrict oneself to the most frequent intonation patterns: a simple falling tone starting on the initial syllable of the last foot in a sentence for statements and WH-questions, and a rising tone for YES-NO questions.

Applied to the selection of phonemes, the frequency criterion would indicate that it is essential to teach the most frequent of all English consonants, [ð], at a very early stage for use in such words as *the*, *this*, and *that*.

Another principle that can be applied to the selection of phonological items, particularly phonemes, is *functional load*. The frequency of a phoneme or phonemic opposition is the number of times that it occurs per thousand words in text. On the other hand, the functional load of a phoneme or phonemic contrast is represented by the number of words in which it occurs in the lexicon, or in the case of a phonemic contrast, the number of pairs of words in the lexicon that it serves to keep distinct. For example, the contrast between the English vowel [i] in *sheep* and [ɪ] in *ship* serves to distinguish many pairs of words (e.g., *peep/pip, peat/pit, peak/pick, peel/pill, peach/ pitch*). The opposition [i/ɪ] has a high functional load. In contrast, the opposition [u/ʊ] in *fool/full* distinguishes very few pairs of words, and thus has a low functional load.

Table 1 lists the functional loads of a number of English phonemic contrasts: initial consonants, final consonants, and vowels. In each list the highest functional load is represented by 100, and the remainder are represented as percentages of this maximum. I suggest that in a course with little time for pronunciation teaching (which is often the case), the teacher might want to concentrate on those phonemic oppositions with a high functional load and give less attention to those with a low functional load.

Table 1. *Relative Functional Load*

Initial Consonants	%	Final Consonants	%	Vowels	%
k/h	100	d/z	100	bit/bat	100
p/b	98	d/l	76	beet/bit	95
p/k	92	n/l	75	bought/boat	88
p/t	87	t/d	72	bit/but	85
p/h, s/h	85	d/n	69	bit/bait	80
l/r	83	l/z	66	cat/cot	76
b/d	82	t/k	65	cat/cut	68
t/k, t/s	81	t/z	61	cot/cut	65
d/l	79	l/n	58	caught/curt	64
p/f	77	t/s	57	coat/curt	63
b/w	76	p/t	43	bit/bet	54
d/r	75	p/k	42.5	bet/bait	53
*h/zero	74	m/n	42	bet/bat, coat/coot	51
t/d	73	s/z	38	cat/cart, beet/boot	50
b/g	71	t/tʃ	31	bet/but, bought/boot	50
f/h	69	k/g	29	hit/hurt	49
f/s	64	*t/θ	27	bead/beard	47
n/l	61	k/tʃ	26	pet/pot	45
m/n	59	b/d	24	hard/hide	44
d/g	56	d/g	23	bet/bite, cart/caught	43
ʃ/h	55	v/z,d/dʒ	22	cart/cur	41

s/ʃ ,d/n	53	b/m, g/ŋ	21	boat/bout	40.5
k/g	50	b/g	20	cut/curt	40
g/w	49	n/ŋ	18	cut/cart	38
n/r	41	p/f,s/θ	17	Kay/care	35
t/tʃ, d/dʒ/	39	dʒ/z,m/v	16	cart/cot	31.5
s/tʃ	37	ŋ/l	15	*here/hair, light/lout	30
g/dʒ	31	p/b,m/ŋ	14	*cot/caught	26
b/v	29	g/dʒ	13	fire/fair	25
*w/hw	27	*tʃ/ʃ	12	her/here, buy/boy	24
*ʃ/tʃ	26	*f/v,*f/θ	9	car/cow	23
*f/v	23	*tʃ/dʒ	8	*her/hair	21
*v/w	22	b/v,s/ʃ,z/ð	7	*tire/tower	19
dʒ/dr, s/θ	21	*θ/ð	6	box/books	18
dʒ/y	20.5	*d/ð	5	*paw/pore	15
*d/ð,*tʃ/dʒ	19	*v/ð	1	pill/pull	13.5
*t/θ	18			pull/pole	12
tʃ/tr	16			bid/beard	11
*f/θ	15			bad/beard	10
*f/hw	13			*pin/pen, *put/putt	9
*v/ð	11			bad/Baird	8
*kw/hw	8			*pull/pool	7
d/z	7			*sure/shore, pooh/poor	5
*s/z	6			*cam/calm, purr/poor	4.5
*tw/kw	5			good/gourd	1
*tw/kw	5				
v/z	2				
*θ/ð/, z/ð	1				

A (*) before an entry indicates that the contrast does not occur in at least one dialectal variety of English.

Supposing one wanted to neglect altogether some oppositions which have a very low functional load, how far down these scales should one go before coming to oppositions that might be regarded as dispensible? In other words, what would be a useful cut-off point? The asterisks before certain oppositions provide a clue. All those contrasts marked with an asterisk do not, in fact, exist in at least one variety of English. Thus the opposition [w/hw] as in *watt/what* is lost in some dialects of English in the U. S. and elsewhere; the oppositions [f/θ] and [v/ð], as in *fin/thin, vie/thy* are lost in some varieties of English (only [f] and [v] occur in some varieties of Cockney, a London dialect, and Black English). The opposition between the vowels of *pin* and *pen* is lost in Southern U.S. English.

With the single exception of the opposition [h/zero], as in *heat/ eat*, which is missing in a number of English dialects, all of these asterisked contrasts are rather low on the scales of functional load—in fact, at about 30% or lower. For our purposes we assume that if native varieties of English can tolerate the loss of one or two oppositions with a functional load of about 30% or less, then in teaching English pronunciation we might decide not to spend the time trying to teach a few difficult phonemic contrasts with a very low functional load. In establishing priorities for the teaching of pronunciation points, one might begin with those having a high functional load.

Arrangement: The Process of Sequencing Pronunciation Teaching Points

In the arrangement, or sequencing, of features of pronunciation it often seems to be assumed that one should first teach the pronunciation of the individual phonemes, leaving problems of rhythm and intonation to be dealt with later, if at all.

My own experience, however, suggests that other arrangements may be more useful. For example, it may be best to begin with rhythm, particularly in teaching English to speakers of languages with a very different kind of rhythm, such as French and Japanese. A possible arrrangement of an English pronunciation course might be as follows.

1. Rhythm, Stress, and Intonation

It might be useful to practice producing feet with varying numbers of syllables, introducing at the same time minimal intonation: two basic tones, falling (for statements and WH-questions) and rising (for YES/NO questions). The following are examples of the kinds of utterances to be practiced in teaching basic rhythm and minimal intonation. The vertical lines indicate divisions between feet, and the bold type represents the *tonic syllable,* that is, where the basic falling or rising tone occurs within the tone group. In this type of exercise, one starts with feet consisting of only one syllable, goes on to feet of two syllables, then varies the number of syllables in the foot. The correct rhythm can be suggested by beating time, always at the rate of one beat per foot.

Chart 2

```
|A|B|C|D|..........|AB|CD|EF|............|AB|C|DEF|G|.....etc.
| Tom | bought | Jane | two | books |
| Tom bought | Jane two | books |
| Tom bought | Jane two | books |
|     Tom     | bought Jane | two books |
| Tom  bought  Jane | two   books | ..........etc.
```

2. Consonants: Syllable Openings and Closings

Here we deal primarily with syllable-initial and syllable-final consonants and consonant clusters. The distinction between syllable initial and syllable final is extremely important when we are dealing with speakers of languages which, unlike English, have a different consonant inventory in these two positions. For them, the learning problem is quite different for initial and final consonants. We deal with consonants before dealing with vowels, because a reasonably correct pronunciation of consonants is probably more important for intelligible and acceptable English than a correct pronunciation of vowels. For some learners consonants present greater difficulties, requiring longer and more careful practice for some learners.

I do not intend to discuss here specific methods of teaching consonants; however, I would like to stress the following important point. The English consonant clusters that occur initially in syllables all have one important characteristic: They all involve *close transition* between the consonants.

For example, many learners have difficulty pronouncing the following clusters: *pl, pr, py, bl, br, by, tw, dw, kl, kr, kw, gl, gr, gw, my, fl, fr, fy, vy*. Such clusters are heterorganic in that the successive consonants are articulated by different organs or different parts of the same organ. This can be termed *articulatory overlap* with the articulation of the second consonant formed before the articulation of the first consonant is released. These clusters can be taught by telling the learner to form the second consonant first. This piece of *applied phonetics* (utilizing our knowledge of the phonetic fact of articulatory overlap) sounds unusual, but it is quite an effective way of getting people unfamiliar with English consonant clusters to pronounce them correctly.

The remaining English consonant clusters, *tr, dr, ky, gy, ny, θr, ʃr*, and those beginning with *s*, that is, *sp, st, sk, sm, sn, sf, sw, spl, spr, spy, str, skl, skr, skw, sky*, present slightly different, but not difficult, problems.

3. Consonants: Open Transistion

Having taught close transition between consonants in clusters, the next problem is to teach the contrasting *open transition* between consonants that is usually regarded as a short, unstressed vowel. I am referring to such contrasting pairs as *tr* versus *t·r* (where [·] represents the extremely brief open transition between the consonants) as in *train* versus *terrain*, *pl* versus *p·l* in *plight* versus *polite*, *kl* versus *k·l* as in *claps* versus *collapse*, *lp* versus *l·p* as in *scalp* versus *scallop*, and so forth. Since many foreign learners of English tend to give far too much weight to these very short unstressed "schwa" vowels, it is important to emphasize that these are not really vowels, but only brief open transitions between consonants.

4. Vowels and Diphthongs

In sequencing pronunciation points for an instructional program, the fourth and final feature of focus is vowels and diphthongs — the syllabic nuclei. Continuing attention can be given to rhythm and intonation, consonantal articulation, and syllabic transition as attention moves to the vowels and diphthongs of the syllabic nucleus.

The Presentation Process:
Five Principles for Pronunciation Instruction

In the presentation of features of pronunciation, five principles of special importance are: (a) precise description; (b) concentration on basics, not symptoms; (c) silent introspection and practice; (d) utilization of all sounds known to the students; and (e) use of imitation and slowed-down speech.

1. Precise Description

A precise description of a sound must follow exacting criteria. It must be accurate and sufficiently detailed so that, if followed, it cannot fail to guide the student to the correct pronunciation. For example, consider the English consonants [f] and [v]; these sounds are generally described in textbooks as *labiodental*. This is accurate as far as it goes, and in many cases it may be enough to instruct the learner to place the lower lip against the upper teeth. This instruction, however, may be inadequate for learners whose native language has no labiodental sounds. I have found that if you tell Japanese speakers to place the lower lip against the upper teeth, they may fold their lower lip backwards and inwards, making contact between the backs of the upper teeth and the outer part of the lower lip. To avoid such errors the instruction must be more detailed, that is, place the inner part of the lower lip against the edges of the upper teeth. It is essential to describe these sounds not merely as labiodental but as *endolabiodental* (i.e., involving the inner part of the lower lip).

2. Concentration on Basics

In saying "teach basics, not symptoms" I have in mind the fact that the most obvious aspect of a sound may, in reality, be superficial — a symptom of some deeper, more important, underlying feature. For example, in English the voiceless stop consonants, *p, t, k,* are *aspirated* preceding a stressed vowel. The most definitive feature of aspiration is the delayed onset of voicing which can be described as a little puff of breath represented by the superscript *h* in $[p^h]$ $[t^h]$ $[k^h]$. But this puff of breath is not the whole story, rather this aspiration is symptomatic. During the articulation of the closed phase of these voiceless aspirated stops, the glottis is wide open. As it takes a little time for the glottis to be narrowed sufficiently for the vocal cords to start vibrating, the onset of voicing is delayed for a fraction of a second. In *unaspirated* stops, on the other hand, the glottis is in a nearly closed position during the stop, and consequently the vocal cords are ready to spring into vibration the instant the release of the closure allows air to flow through the glottis. In other words, the basic distinction between aspirated and unaspirated voiceless stops is the configuration of the glottis during the stop phase.

Aspirated Stops. How can a teacher utilize this phonetic knowledge in teaching aspirated stops to those who do not have them (e.g., French speakers learning English) and unaspirated stops to those who have only aspirated stops (e.g., English speakers learning French). What the teacher can do in the first case is induce the French speaker to articulate voiceless aspirated stops with the glottis in the wide-open *breath* position. What can be done in the second case is to help the English speaker produce voiceless unaspirated stops with the glottis in the nearly closed *whisper* position.

A useful technique for teaching aspiration can begin by getting the learner to produce a prolonged outflow of breath. Then, while concentrating on keeping the air flowing, ask the learner to superimpose a quick oral closure, [p], [t], or [k]. This may be roughly symbolized as [hhhᵖhhh], where the raised [p] is used to suggest that the oral closure is briefly superimposed on a continuous outgoing breath stream. The important things to suggest to students are that they try to maintain the breath flow and to feel the wide-open glottis throughout the production, especially during the short period when the lips are closed for the [p]. Have the learner say this again and again, shortening the initial stretch of breath little by little and always striving to maintain that feeling of wide-open glottis: [hhhᴾhh], [hhᴾhh], [hᴾhh]. The two next steps are: (a) to drop off the initial [h] altogether, retaining only the feeling of wide-open glottis throughout; and (b) to add on a vowel after the breath flow, which is progressively shortened, [phhha], [phha], [pha].

Unaspirated Stops. Teaching unaspirated [p], [t], [k] can proceed along analogous lines; however, rather than maintaining a prolonged [hhh] throughout the stop, the learner must produce prolonged and maintained whisper, eventually reaching the point where the feeling of whisper is maintained during the stop of [p], [t], [k]. The learner produces silent stops with whisper configuration of the glottis during the stop. The learner can then add a vowel immediately upon release of the stop.

A second example of teaching basics rather than the symptoms involves [θ] and [ð] as in *thin* and *then.* These sounds are usually described as *dental* or *interdental fricatives.* In fact, the dentality of these sounds (i.e., the near approach of the tip and rim of the tongue to the edges of the upper teeth) is largely a secondary effect. A more fundamental characteristic is the relatively flat and spread configuration of the front part of the tongue.

Let us begin by contrasting the production of the flat fricative [θ] with that of grooved fricative [s]. The high-frequency hissing sound of English [s] is produced by channeling the flow of air through a groove formed between the blade of the tongue and the alveolar ridge, and directing the high-velocity jet against the edges of the teeth. A good deal of the hiss noise of [s] derives from the turbulent flow of air past the teeth. In contrast, in the production of [θ] the tongue is in a flat configuration, so that the channel between the tongue and the alveolar ridge is much wider. Consequently, the air flows much more slowly. There is no high-velocity jet striking the teeth, and the resultant friction of [θ] is quieter and lower pitched than the hiss sound of [s].

One can begin to teach [θ] by getting the student to articulate an [s] several times at first aloud and then silently, noting the feeling of the sides of the tongue blade pressing up to the ridge behind the teeth, leaving a very narrow grooved channel. When quite conscious of this feeling, ask the student to allow the tongue to relax and flatten. Having consciously contrasted the feeling of the tense and very narrow channel of [s] with the relaxed, flattened, and wide channel of [θ], the student can try directing an air stream through these two contrasting formations. Ask the student to alternate the sounds [s] and [θ], noting that the resultant gentle wide-channel hiss requires little or no adjustment to turn it into a very acceptable [θ].

Teaching [θ] in this manner emphasizes the fact that [θ] is a flat, wide-channel, low-velocity, quiet hiss, compared to a grooved, narrow-channel, high-velocity loud and noisy hiss of [s]. This teaching technique is at least as effective as concentrating on the secondary characteristic of the proximity of the tongue rim to the edges of the upper teeth. It must be noted that once an articulation has been taught intensive practice of words and phrases containing the sound is required to make its regular use in connected speech automatic.

3. Silent Introspection

We have already touched on the third principle—the use of silent instrospection and practice. It is hardly possible to overemphasize the importance of this. Pronunciation instruction usually concentrates solely on practicing sounds aloud. This is quite understandable since sounds are perceived by the ear and must be said aloud to be heard. However, the sounds of languages are the result of articulatory activities in the vocal tract, and focusing the students attention on these activities can be very helpful. Whenever you make sounds aloud, the auditory impression tends to mask or override the sensations of muscle movements, the proprioceptive sensations. Yet student awareness of these proprioceptive sensations can be a useful adjunct to making the articulatory adjustments necessary for learning the articulation of new sounds.

Silent introspection about sounds provides a starting point for proceeding from the known to the unknown in learning new articulations. We saw an example of this in the development of lax, wide-channel [θ] from tense, narrow-channel [s]. Another example is the teaching of [ʃ] from [s] to persons who lack this kind of distinction in their own language (e.g., Spanish speakers).

In preparing to teach the [s] and [ʃ] distinction the teacher should begin by first *isolating* the [s] of *see* and the [ʃ] of *she*. A teacher's ability to lift any articulation out of its normal environment, without altering it in the slightest, is a very valuable skill. Having isolated [s] and [ʃ], alternate them slowly and deliberately many times once or twice aloud and then silently. With a little introspection the learner can note that the articulation of [ʃ] is a little further back than that of [s]. At the same time the learner will probably be aware that the lips are in a neutral or spread position for [s], but are slightly rounded for [ʃ]. Introspecting more intensively, ask the student to feel the tip and rim of the tongue lightly touching the backs of the lower teeth for [s]. This contact is broken when the tongue is slightly shifted back for [ʃ]. A teacher who has clearly felt this important articulatory difference is in a more informed position for teaching it than one who has not.

A similar technique can be used in teaching Spanish speakers. Although Spanish has no post-alveolar fricative [ʃ], they do have a post-aveolar affricate [tʃ]. Learners can be guided to introspect silently about its articulation and apply the knowledge thus acquired to their production of [ʃ].

The teacher can experiment with many other sounds, and employ silent articulation to learn how various sounds are produced and can be deliberately manipulated. For example, silent alternation of the tense and lax vowels [i] and [ɪ], as in *beet* and *bit*, is quite revealing. By studying vowels silently, one can attach a genuine, introspectively experienced meaning to such labels as front, back, high, and low.

Through silent articulatory experimentation, the ability to round and unround any vowel at will can be acquired. Keeping the tongue in a rigidly fixed position, the learner can slowly and deliberately add or remove lip rounding. Not only is this skill useful to the English speaker in acquiring the pronunciation of rounded front vowels in French or the unrounded, high, central to back vowels in Russian and Turkish, but it is often useful to teach it to learners of English. A first approximation to the difficult vowel of *bird*, for example, can sometimes be taught by having the student unround a back [o].

4. Utilization of Known Sounds

The fourth principle is the utilization of all sounds known to the students. Teachers should resist being influenced by conventional or stereotypical views on the teaching of pronunciation, and thus fail to take advantage of the articulatory possibilities of their students. For example, knowing that the French [i] and [u] sounds are too tense and close to serve as English [ɪ] and [ʊ] in *pit* and *put*, we can capitalize instead on the fact that French has the more open vowels *é* and *o* (in *été* and *moto*). Although these vowels do not occur in closed syllables in French, it is quite easy to teach a French speaker to use them for the English vowels. They may not be perfect, but they are much better substitutes than the tense French [i] and [u].

Many years ago when I was teaching at a short summer course in Rumania, I observed that my students consistently mispronounced the (British, RP) vowel of *bird*. They pronounced it as something like [berd] with a trilled [r]. However, I also had noticed that in their own language there was a vowel that was almost identical to the English "bird" vowel, written as *a*. It only occurred short in Rumanian, but I found that by writing *bǎǎd* with two *ǎ's* and asking them to read it I could induce my students to pronounce an almost perfect *bird*.

Another example involves speakers of the Dravidian language Tamil. Like speakers of many other Indian languages, Tamil speakers generally use a trilled [r] in speaking English. This appears to be largely a matter of convention, supported by the orthographic and orthoepic facts that trilled [r]'s of Indian languages are normally transliterated with *r*. Consequently the letter *r* is associated with trilled [r]. What is overlooked is that in some dialects of Tamil there is a sound, heard in the middle of the word *paṟam* "fruit," which is similar to a typical American [r] and is a much better sound to use in teaching English.

Further, most people are aware of dialectal differences in their own language, and they can often imitate dialectal sounds. It is useful for pronunciation teachers to study the dialects of their students' language, since such information can be useful in teaching English sounds. For example, although Athenian Greek does not have the [ʃ] or [tʃ] sounds in English *ship* and *chip*, several other Greek dialects do. These can be taught by asking an Athenian to imitate the Cretan pronunciation of the greeting *xairete* or the word *kai* "hand," which begin with [ʃ] and [tʃ] respectively in Cretan pronunciation.

Finally, everyone can make all sorts of "nonlanguage" sounds. These can sometimes serve as a basis to build the articulation of foreign sounds by conscious introspective experimentation.

For example, deep velar or uvular articulations are foreign to American English, but most Americans are familiar with the exclamation of disgust — *yecch*! That word contains a voiceless uvular fricative or trill. Another source of uvular articulation upon which the teacher can build is gargling. The articulation of a gargle is uvular, and it can be a useful basis for acquiring a uvular trill or fricative.

Surprisingly, a gargle can sometimes be used as a starting point for the acquisition of a certain rather common type of American [r] or the vowel in *bird*. This type of [r] has the whole body of the tongue bunched up in the mouth with a hollow or furrow in it at approximately the velar articulatory zone. This furrow is quite like the furrow in the back of the tongue in which the uvula vibrates in the articulation of a uvular trill. Consequently, one can arrive at this type of American [r] as follows. Produce a prolonged gargle or uvular trill; stop the sound, but continue to hold precisely the same tongue configuration. Do this several times taking care to get the feeling of that tongue configuration, noting particularly the sensation of the furrow in the center line of the back of the tongue. Now, holding that articulatory posture produce voice, but no trilling of the uvula. With a few deliberate adjustments of the tongue posture, one should arrive at a sound closely resembling a type of American [r] or "bird" vowel.

5. *Imitation and Slowed-Down Speech*

The fifth principle is imitation and slowed-down speech. Firstly, the pronunciation teacher should cultivate the skill of imitation in order to produce as exact a replication as possible of one's students' pronunciation. By exactly imitating a mispronunciation, the teacher may be able to analyse and discover what is wrong with it. Furthermore, it is helpful to students to encourage them to listen to an accurate imitation of their mispronunciation contrasted with the correct pronunciation.

Secondly, slowed-down speech is also useful to cultivate. One cannot expect students at an early stage in learning a language to pick up details of pronunciation from rapid or normal speech. On the other hand, the slowed-down speech of an unskilled teacher will normally contain numerous distortions. What one has to do is to practice assiduously saying words, short phrases, and longer sentences at a very slow tempo, but retaining, as far as possible, all the pronunciation features of normal or fast speech. The teacher who does this must be very conscious of the intonation, the rhythm, and the sounds of the normal pronunciation. In slowing down one must be very careful to keep the relative pitches of successive syllables as they were; to keep the relative durations of the slowed-down ("stretched") syllables the same as they were; and to retain all the "weak" pronunciations, the ultrashort open transitions of the original becoming short, central "schwa" vowels. This takes practice, but it can be done and is very useful.

Conclusion

It is sometimes thought that using phonetics in teaching pronunciation means using phonetic transcription, clearly that is a very inadequate view of what it means to use phonetics in teaching. In the preceding paper I have given a brief accounting of what it really means to "use phonetics." It means to use the knowledge and, above all, the skills of the phonetician whenever possible.

I emphasized that teaching pronunciation is teaching a motor skill. It is teaching students to do something: to produce sounds, not merely to listen. You cannot teach guitar by making students listen to guitar music. You have to teach them precisely what to do with their fingers. In much the same way you cannot teach pronunciation by making students listen to speech. You have to teach them precisely what to do with their vocal organs. The most effective way to do this is through intensive silent experimentation in the vocal tract. I have made a great point of this because it is so rarely practised: Making sounds silently is one of the most important keys to the successful teaching of pronunciation.

References

Catford, J. C. (1966, May). English phonology and the teaching of pronunciation. *College English,* pp. 605-613.

Catford, J. C. (1985). Rest and open transition in a systemic phonology of English. In *Systemic perspectives on discourse: Vol. 1. Selected papers from the 9th international systemic workshop* (pp. 333-348). Norwood, NJ: Ablex.

The Pronunciation Monitor: L2 Acquisition Considerations and Pedagogical Priorities

William W. Crawford

Georgetown University

Editorial Notes

In "The Pronunciation Monitor: L2 Acquisition Considerations and Pedagogical Priorities," William W. Crawford reviews and summarizes significant issues that impinge on pronunciation instructional theory and practice in ESL/EFL, and indeed, more broadly, on all of modern language teaching today.

In the first part of the paper Crawford reviews pertinent literature on pronunciation and second language learning/second language acquisition perspectives. He discusses controversial issues in detail with reference to some of the work of (in order of presentation): Lenneberg, Scovel, Neufeld, Tarone, Hill, Guiora, Heyde, Krashen, Rosansky, Terrell, Stern, and Bialystok. Topics include:

A Critical Period for Learning Language?
Krashen: Monitor Model Hypothesis
Pronunciation Skills and the Monitor Model
Bialystok: A Theoretical Model of L2 Learning

Crawford then turns his attention to theoretical and pedagogical concerns in the teaching of pronunciation. His review of the literature in this area draws upon some of the work of (in order of presentation): Morley, Strevens, Parish, Prator, Abraham, Stevick, Stockwell and Bowen, Shen, Fries, and Acton. Topics include:

Can Pronunciation be Taught?
Focus on the Learner: Needs and Goals
The Learner's Role
Pedagogical Priorities
Priorities and the Teacher's Role
Priorities and Program Planning
Teacher Preparation

Pedagogical priorities are discussed in detail, and important considerations for teacher training are suggested. He does not recommend a set formula of pedagogical priorities, but suggests that flexible priorities must be based on the assessment of student needs and goals of each class, and therefore, vary accordingly.

J.M.

The Pronunciation Monitor: L2 Acquisition Considerations and Pedagogical Priorities

Drawing upon information from linguistics, psychology, sociology, and other related fields over the last 20 years, applied linguistics has emerged as a bonafide discipline with independent theoretical models and a growing body of research. Within applied linguistics, second language (L2) acquisition has been the most active area of scholarly inquiry. Overall, however, the specific area of interlanguage (IL) phonology has been largely neglected in L2 research. Tarone (1978) suggests that one reason for this neglect may be the commonly held belief that the learner's L2 pronunciation is influenced more strongly by negative transfer from the first language than is the learner's IL grammar. However, she also notes that transfer is only a small part of the influence on IL phonology.

Recently, interest in IL phonology and the development of new approaches to the teaching of L2 pronunciation has renewed. A review of literature[1] reveals that attention has focused on four areas of research: (a) aptitude or ability, (b) child and adult L2 phonological acquisition, (c) processes (and constraints) operative in shaping IL phonology, and (d) methods of instruction for learners whose pronunciation appears amenable to change despite evidence of "fossilization."

A Critical Period for Learning Language?

A theme that recurs throughout the literature on L2 phonology is the concern with one fundamental question: Is it possible for (adult) learners to attain native-like L2 pronunciation?

In an attempt to answer this question, researchers initially turned to Lenneberg's (1967) *The Biological Foundation of Language*, in which his critical period hypothesis asserts that with lateralization the brain somehow loses it capacity for language learning. The degree to which this loss affects all areas of L2 competence varies according to strong and weak versions of this theory. In general, however, those who hold this viewpoint tend to agree that with lateralization, ability in L2 pronunciation is affected more than syntax or vocabulary.

Scovel (1969), an early proponent of this view, claims[2] that no adult ever achieves perfect native pronunciation in an L2. While the adult learner often surpasses the younger learner in mastering vocab-

ulary, syntax, and stylistic variations, according to Scovel adults cannot master pronunciation with native fluency.

Attributing limited ability in L2 pronunciation to cerebral dominance has received considerable criticism. Neufeld (1980) asks "Is
the language learning disability of adults psycholinguistic or psycho-
motor in nature" (p. 286)? In a large body of data, Neufeld found
little evidence of the *language acquisition device* (LAD) in older
learners. He found that a neurophysiologically-induced language learning disability was largely unsupported, and that the only consistent
indicator of adult inferiority was lack of native-like pronunciation.
The disability, if one exists, may be less psycholinguistic than psycho-
motor in nature. The adult learner may know how the target pronunciation should sound, but cannot get his vocal apparatus to obey
cerebral instructions. Tarone (1978) further adds that the psychomo-
tor explanation for phonological fossilization would suggest that the
nerves and muscles necessary for pronunciation of the new L2 patterns are no longer flexible, so that native-like pronunciation is
impossible.

However, we should hasten to point out that both Tarone and
Neufeld refute the argument that native-like L2 pronunciation is
impossible. According to Neufeld (1980), "as demonstrated in the
1979 study, some older learners do attain a native-like command of
phonological rules, prosodic features and articulatory skills in their
second language" (p. 269). This view is further supported by earlier
studies in which Neufeld (1977) experimented with methods of teaching L2 pronunciation which proved to be successful in helping adults
to acquire native or near-native proficiency in L2 pronunciation.

A second kind of criticism of the role played by cerebral dominance in the acquisition of L2 pronunciation comes from an anthropological perspective. Hill (1970) asserted that fossilization of L2
phonology is by no means inevitable, claiming that closer attention
should be given to cultural rather than biological factors as its cause.
She supports this position through anthropological evidence that native peoples, like the Vaupes Indians of the Amazon and the Siane of
New Guinea, learn several languages as adults and achieve native-
like fluency.

The third type of criticism of lateralization theory is one that relies
on the affective argument and focuses on the role of empathy in L2
learners. This position attributes L2 phonological disability to an
essential lack of empathy with the native speakers and culture of the
L2. Those who support this position (Guiora, Beit-Hallami, Brannon,
Dull, & Scovel, 1972; Heyde, 1977) claim that the more sensitive
one is to the feelings and behavior of others, the more likely one is to
perceive the subtleties and unique aspects of the second language

and incorporate them in speech. That is, the more empathetic people are, the more authentically they will pronounce a second language. These researchers find socio-economic factors especially powerful in determining the degree of empathy, hence proficiency, in L2 pronunciation and feel that they provide very strong directions for future research.

The final and perhaps most significant criticism of cerebral dominance comes from cognitive psychology. Krashen (1977) and Rosansky (1975) both observe that the close of the critical period is directly related to the onset of Piaget's stage of formal operations. This viewpoint parallels the distinction between acquisition and learning proposed by Krashen's *monitor model theory.* This position, discussed widely in current ESL literature, has given us an interesting perspective on the processes involved in L2 acquisition, yet it fails to provide a satisfactory explanation for the role of pronunciation within its framework. Implications for language learning and teaching from the monitor model — and pedagogical model called *the natural approach* — will be the focus of our discussion of the pronunciation monitor.

Krashen: A Monitor Model Hypothesis

The monitor model hypothesis claims that competence is developed in L2 in one of two ways, via (1) acquisition or *implicit linguistic knowledge*[3], a natural process similar to that observed in children acquiring their first language system; and (2) learning or *explicit linguistic knowledge,* which is a process associated with the classroom, in which pedagogical rules are consciously represented and attention is focused on form. However, for Krashen (1981) "acquisition is more central than language learning in L2 performance" (p. 101). According to Krashen, learning is available to the adult performer in L2 production only as a *monitor* (self-correction device) operating on previously acquired linguistic information, while acquisition is characterized as intuitive, automatic, and spontaneous. L2 utterances can only be initiated from the acquired system.

This view of L2 acquisition (Krashen & Terrell, 1983) is based on the single premise that language is acquired in only one way: by "understanding messages." Language acquisition occurs when we obtain *comprehensible input,* when we understand what we hear or read in another language. Therefore, the prerequisite for L2 acquisition is our understanding (and internalizing) what is being said (content). Attention to how the message is transmitted (form) is of secondary importance and relegated to the lesser role of L2 learning. For Krashen and Terrell (1983) this creates the "great paradox of language teaching." In their words, "language is best taught when it is being used to transmit messages, not when it is explicitly taught for conscious learning" (p. 55).

For Krashen, conscious learning is necessarily secondary to the primary goal of L2 acquisition and is available for use only in monitoring L2 production. This notion of an internal monitoring device, which uses conscious language learning for purposes of self-correction, is central to our discussion of the teaching and learning of L2 pronunciation skills. The function of conscious learning, according to Krashen and Terrell (1983), is even more limited when we consider that monitoring one's speech successfully requires the following conditions: (a) the L2 user has to have time to examine the utterance before it is spoken, (b) the speaker has to be consciously concerned with correctness, and (c) the speaker has to know the rule. These conditions rarely occur in natural speech, which tends to place primary attention on what is being said not how it is being said.

Conscious learning, according to Krashen and Terrell (1983), is used ideally to supplement acquired competence via the monitor, supplying aspects of language that have not yet been acquired. These aspects may not add a great deal to the communicative value of the utterance; however, they will enhance the overall impression of the output, "they may give it a more polished, a more 'educated' look" (p. 19).

From a pedagogical perspective, a major goal of the natural approach (Krashen & Terrell, 1983) is to produce "efficient users," that is, those who can monitor their speech without interrupting the flow of communication. Krashen and Terrell detail the individual use of the monitor for three types of language learners:

1. Monitor over-users are those who monitor all the time. Monitor over-users are constantly checking their output with their learned conscious knowledge of the second language.

2. Monitor under-users are L2 performers who do not seem to use the Monitor to any extent, even when conditions encourage it . . . Under-users do not rely on conscious rules, but only on acquisition.

3. The optimal monitor user is the adult L2 performer who uses the Monitor when it is appropriate, when it does not get in the way of communication . . . Optimal monitor users can therefore use their learned competence as a supplement to their acquired competence. (pp. 44-45)

Pronunciation Skills and the Monitor Model

Regarding the acquisition of L2 pronunciation skills from the perspective of the monitor model, "the important variables determining pronunciation accuracy in English are all acquisition variables" (Purcell & Suter, 1980, p. 286). In other words, according to Krashen and Terrell (1983), pronunciation ability, or a good accent, may be largely dependent on what has been acquired, not on rules which have been learned. Krashen questions whether pronunciation can even be taught or learned. Citing the work of Purcell and Suter (1980) who maintain that "teachers and classrooms have remarkably little to do with how well our students [pronounce] English" (p. 285), Krashen and Terrell claim that classroom exercises have limited value.

This view leads Krashen and Terrell to the conclusion that if classroom instruction has a limited effect on pronunciation, the teacher can best serve the students by providing a comfortable environment for students to acquire and practice English. No specific activities are recommended in their natural approach.

If we are to believe the central hypothesis of the monitor model, this would mean that L2 pronunciation strategies are acquired in only one way: by understanding messages or comprehensible input. However, this explanation seems less than satisfying. Even Krashen and Terrell (1983) point out that comprehensible input, although necessary, is not sufficient for acquisition; there are affective prerequisites to acquisition. In addition to those variables outlined in Stern's (1975) portrait of the "good language learner," which stresses heavily the role of the monitor in L2 acquisition, researchers have isolated other variables: concern for pronunciation accuracy, aptitude for oral mimicry (Purcell & Suter, 1980), as well as involvement in emotional experiences and perception of emotional expression.

Personal observation of my gradual acquisition of Japanese syntax and vocabulary over a 2-year period supports the claim that we "acquire language by understanding input that is a little beyond our current level of (acquired) competence" (Krashen & Terrell, 1983, p.32). I am convinced that pronunciation improves through gradual monitoring of the acquired system based on conscious knowledge of the facts learned about the language.

Bialystok: A Theoretical Model of L2 Learning

From a theoretical perspective, it would seem that Krashen has underestimated the role of conscious learning within the monitoring device as an active L2 acquisition mechanism. This notion is implicit in an alternative theoretical model of L2 learning proposed by

Bialystok, who claims that acquisition may also occur via transfer of information from explicit linguistic knowledge (learning) to implicit linguistic knowledge (acquisition). While the theoretical models proposed by Bialystok and Krashen are similar in many respects, Krashen maintains that conscious learning is available for use only in the monitor and is unavailable as a means of L2 acquisition.

For Bialystok (1978) the difference between explicit and implicit linguistic knowledge is defined operationally. As she explains, *explicit linguistic knowledge* contains all conscious information about the language and the ability to articulate that information, including grammar, lexical items, pronunciation rules, and so forth. *Implicit linguistic knowledge* is the unconscious, intuitive knowledge, used automatically and spontaneously, upon which the language learner operates in order to produce responses in the target language.

Bialystok concurs with Krashen regarding the function of the monitor in L2 acquisition, claiming that conscious knowledge of the language may be used for examination, modification, or correction of output. However, the theoretical construct posited by Bialystok differs from Krashen's model in one significant aspect: "after continued use, [explicit] information may become automatic and transferred to Implicit Linguistic Knowledge, but the initial encounter, because of its explicitness, requires that it is represented in Explicit Knowledge" (1978, p. 72).

Bialystok (1978) stresses the primacy of acquisition in her discussion of implicit linguistic knowledge, claiming that the purpose of the language learning enterprise is to increase the amount of implicit knowledge, since fluency is a function of that knowledge. While for Krashen formal language learning is not a viable means for acquiring L2 (including pronunciation), Bialystok encourages the use of language drills and exercises which familiarize the learner with previously learned information. In this regard she states, "the type of formal practice described here addresses itself to the question of [L2 acquisition] by allowing information to move from Explicit Linguistic Knowledge to the operating store in Implicit Linguistic Knowledge" (p. 77).

Can Pronunciation be Taught?

Regardless of which theoretical view of L2 acquisition one elects, the question remains: Can pronunciation be taught? Weighing current thoughts on theory against pedagogical concerns, Morley (1975) points out that the concept of teaching pronunciation is valid if the teacher wants students who can mimic, while the teacher modifies or corrects. However, if the desired result is the use of spoken English with sufficient intelligibility that it does not interfere with communication, then the concept must be the learning, not the teaching of spoken English.

To this end, Strevens (1984) observes with elegant simplicity: "Teaching works. . . It is difficult to see how a person could remain a teacher if he or she did not believe this. Of course not *all* teaching *always* helps learning. But what I am calling *informed teaching* can work and usually does" (p. 2). In Strevens' integrated model of language learning/teaching process, he elaborates on the role of teaching in the process of L2 acquisition:

> Teaching, of itself, does not cause learning. Equally, the mechanisms of comprehension and learning of themselves, cannot attain the relatively rapidly and closely-specified goals of language learning. But informed language teaching can accelerate learning and guide it to chosen goals by deliberately and intentionally assisting each of the many mechanisms of learning as they become relevant throughout the learner's process. These mechanisms of learning include the presence of qualities such as impact, interest, variety and the optimum organization of the learning intake; but the core of the mechanisms lies in a wide range of mental processes—that is, roughly, cognitive strategies, or modes of thinking—available to every learner and capable of being assisted through informed teaching. Informed teaching can speed up and make more effective the learner's ability to comprehend and learn. (p. 4)

If we accept Strevens' compelling logic that teaching does indeed work and furthermore that it facilitates L2 acquisition, then we can finally begin to address ourselves to the practical concerns of the classroom. However, this is no simple matter either. Parish (1977) observes that the pronunciation teaching in the ESOL classroom is more complicated than is usually suggested in teacher training coursework. This complexity, Parish asserts, consists of appropriately combining the linguistic knowledge and specific pedagogical techniques of the teacher with a sensitivity to the point of view of the learner, including a reasonable expectation of progress, attention to the learners classroom behavior, and a proportionate importance of pronunciation to the entire language learning process.

Focus on the Learner: Needs and Role

In this regard, we are in complete agreement with Krashen and Terrell's (1983) assertion that the selection of methods and materials to be used in a class must be based on the defined goals of that class, and that those goals must be based on an assessment of the students' needs.

However, in most situations students enrolled in ESL classes are expected to conform to the goals of the program, rather than the program conforming to the needs of the students. ESL teachers all too often establish their goals from a pedagogical perspective, organizing their classes around those items they feel most important to teach. This backwards approach to efficient and successful L2 acquisition attributes only secondary importance to the larger question of learning, and all but ignores student needs.

The neglect of student needs in establishing pedagogical priorities in the ESL classroom is a serious shortcoming in the field today. We must approach each class with the single goal of meeting the needs of the class as a whole as well as its individual members. Therefore, an ESL curriculum must be based on priorities that are unique to each classroom and linked to such practical matters as age, sex, ability-level, linguistic background, professional and personal goals, and duration of the course. No class should be taught in the same manner twice or should use the same material, as the goals of each class should vary according to student needs. Furthermore, since the goals of each class are based ideally on assessment of student needs, no clear-cut, rigid set of priorities can be offered for use in all teaching situations. Specific pedagogical priorities must vary with student needs. At best, we can only offer general guidelines for most situations. Establishing priorities based on an assessment of student needs obviates the need for student evaluation. Most programs test students for purposes of placement: evaluating their abilities in grammar, reading, writing, and listening. However, students' spoken skills (fluency or accuracy) are seldom tested. If the goal is to provide flexible priorities for the pronunciation class, testing cannot be considered a luxury, undertaken only as time allows.

In addition to a set of flexible priorities based on analysis of student needs, two goals can serve as general guidelines for all ESL pronunciation classes regardless of individual differences. They are intelligibility and speech awareness. While researchers continue to debate the degree to which L2 learners acquire native-like fluency in L2 pronunciation, intelligibility must be the minimum goal for the classroom. In the past it was often felt that complete accuracy was necessary for student success. Today most teachers have adopted a more moderate view with intelligibility as a primary goal, rather than native-like mastery of the L2 sound system. Beyond intelligibility, as Morley points out, "we are aiming for the best possible operational English accent for individual speakers of other languages" (personal communication, 1985).

Along these lines, Prator (1971) adds that in the absence of any consensus regarding the degree of accuracy to be sought in teaching pronunciation, most teachers will choose an intermediate position between absolute allophonic accuracy and rough phonemic approximation. From a pedagogical point of view this would mean that the teacher must establish a system of priorities, determining the elements of pronunciation that will be emphasized, and those that will be handled briefly.

The second priority crucial to the acquisition of L2 phonology is speech awareness on the part of the language learner. This is largely accomplished through the instruction of self- and peer-monitoring techniques.

Abraham (1984) keenly observes that while acquisition (in Krashen's terms) may be the more important process, it does not necessarily lead to correct usage required in academic settings, where deviation from the standard form conveys the impression of lack of education. Therefore, he continues, many teachers feel the need to stress rules and encourage use of learned knowledge via the monitor. Based on statistical evidence from empirical studies, Abraham concludes that it is helpful to encourage monitoring in academic settings.

According to Bialystok's (1978) model of L2 acquisition, in addition to explicit linguistic knowledge (Krashen's learning) which is available for use (only) in the language monitor, information that is represented in implicit linguistic knowledge may be made conscious or explicit for purposes of monitoring. This is especially significant for adult L2 learners whose monitoring—including auditory, tactile, or visual dimensions—tends to diminish over time.

In this way, both explicit and implicit linguistic knowledge are available for use in monitoring. Furthermore, if we believe that, according to Bialystok's model, information that is stored in explicit linguistic knowledge may become automatic and transferred to implicit linguistic knowledge after continued use via the monitor, then both learning and acquisition are significant factors in the language learning process. To this end, monitoring plays a crucial role in L2 acquisition that cannot be ignored.

The Learner's Role

Unfortunately, as we are reminded by Morley (1975), very little of the available material encourages students to take an active role in their learning. Morley asserts that often students are not cognitively involved in their learning; performative involvement is monitored by someone else (i.e., teacher correction), and students are seldom shown how to monitor their own speech performance.

On the other hand, we cannot ignore Abraham's (1984) warning that the student's ability to consciously apply rules—to monitor his speech—is limited. The teacher must be cautioned not to have unrealistic expectations about the amount of monitoring a student can do. Fortunately, as conscious learning is transferred to the acquired system via the monitor, only the most salient, unacquired aspects of L2 phonology are involved in the monitoring process at any one time.

Pedagogical Priorities

The search for pedagogical priorities is not a new issue within applied linguistics. Much of Fries' *Teaching and Learning English as a Foreign Language* (1945) is based on a set of pedagogical priorities implicit throughout his work. Such goals are clearly evident in his outline of the pronunciation materials included in an intensive course in English for Latin Americans.

Likewise, Stockwell and Bowen (1965) make explicit the criteria upon which they determined the sequence of their presentation of the sounds of English and Spanish: (a) hierarchy of difficulty, (b) functionality, (c) potential mishearing, and (d) pattern congruity. Based on these criteria, Stockwell and Bowen offer specific priorities for the classroom in the form of a *preferred pedagogical sequence:*

1. Basic intonation features and patterns (including stress, pitch, juncture, and rhythm)
2. Weak stressed vowels
3. Strong stressed vowels and diphthongs
4. Voiced stop-spirants
5. Vibrants and liquids
6. Voiced stops
7. Spirants
8. Nasals and palatals
9. Semivowels
10. Consonant clusters
11. Other intonation features and patterns (p. 17)

Similarly, leaders in the field of ESL pronunciation—including Prator, Parish, Morley, and Stevick—have addressed the need for establishing specific priorities for the ESL pronunciation classroom.

Prator is perhaps the first figure in applied linguistics to directly tackle the question of pedagogical priorities for the ESL/EFL classroom. In his much overlooked article, "Phonetics vs. Phonemics in the ESL Classroom: When is Allophonic Accuracy Important?" (1971), he arrives at a four-level hierarchy of priorities based on

structuralist concepts, which can be applied when dealing with pronunciation errors caused by interference from the students' native
language. In his heirarchy, priority is assigned, from highest to lowest,
to the teaching of:

1. Suprasegmental phonemes
2. Segmental phonemes
3. Allophones in complementary distribution
4. Allophones in free alternation (p. 69)

Upon first examination such a heirarchy might appear simplistic,
suggesting that English phonology consists of a set of discrete phonemes strung together. However, closer examination reveals close
attention to the importance of the role of allophonic variation in
providing "acoustical clues to the recognition of phonemes" (Shen,
1959). If we maintain the primacy of intelligibility in the establishing
of pedagogical priorities for the pronunciation class, then Prator's
(1971) advice is still worthy of careful consideration. Prator cautions
that more information is needed regarding the value of features, such
as aspiration and vowel length as clues to word recognition. Further,
he warns the teacher that any departure from the phonemic norm
can have a negative effect on the intelligibility of speech. In this
respect, he regards unintelligibility as "the cumulative effect of many
little departures from the phonemic norms of the language" (p. 61).
The departures may be allophonic or phonemic, but under certain
circumstances, he concludes, any abnormality of speech can contribute to unintelligibility.

While Prator's research makes an important first attempt at establishing a set of priorities, it fails to provide room for characteristic
phonetic features of English (vowel reduction, assimilation, syllable
restructuring, palatalization, etc.) which play key roles in English
phonology. Such information must be incorporated into any comprehensive syllabus for the ESL/EFL pronunciation classroom. Among
some oriental languages, for example, the role of lip posturing is a
major obstacle in the acquisition of English pronunciation both in
terms of intelligibility and native-like accent. For speakers of Japanese and Chinese, this phonetic characteristic of English should merit
a high priority in the pronunciation class as attention to this single
feature of English can have sweeping results when successfully taught.
Conscious learning of lip posturing is initially important for use in the
pronunciation monitor; it is significant later as it automatizes and
transfers from explicit language knowledge to the acquired system in
terms of implicit language knowledge.

Priorities and the Teacher's Role

More recently, other researchers such as Parish (1977) have gone so far as to offer a *practical philosophy of pronunciation,* based on six specific methodological principles and a 10-point pedagogical approach derived from long-term observation and supervision of ESL teachers. This practical philosophy is intended to provide a perspective for the teacher, not only in pronunciation, but in every aspect of language learning. Parish believes that this perspective must be the basis for any technique or methodology, and that it ultimately validates or invalidates any specific procedure. Parish also offers the following approach to teaching pronunciation:

1. Tact in correction
2. Frequency in correction
3. Intensity in correction
4. Importance of exact imitation
5. Compromise in correction
6. Simplicity of explanation
7. Sound/letter correspondence
8. Preciseness in correction
9. Contrastive information
10. Dialect relativity (p. 314)

Stevick (1978) questions this practical philosophy of pronunciation with another view: "The learning of pronunciation involves neuromuscular and some cognitive activity, but it also has affective and social components, which carry important implications for the role of the teacher" (p.145). In this regard, we agree with Stevick's view that the instruction of L2 pronunciation skills must be seen as only one aspect of a total process, which involves the whole learner and not just the speech apparatus or cognitive faculties. Acton (1984) lends further strength to the position taken by Stevick claiming that we must think of the process of pronunciation change as having an inside-out dimension. He claims that we have sound theoretical justification for attempting to enhance the learner's development of an "English-language ego" (p. 75) which enables the learner to mimic native speakers behaviors of various kinds.

Priorities and Program Planning

Priorities, such as those described above, play an increasingly important role in the ESL classroom, forming the core upon which curriculum is built. The University of Michigan's English Language

Institute (Morley, 1979; 1985; in press) has pioneered recent trends in the development of modern pronunciation techniques and materials used as part of its Pronunciation Laboratory Program, which aims, in addition to the minimal goal of intelligibility, at developing creative speech awareness in the learner. According to Morley (1975), one of the characteristics of such a program is classes in which students are cognitively involved and are apprised of what they are doing, and why they are doing it. Such a methodology concurs with Krashen and Terrell's (1983) natural approach, which maintains that course goals should be specified, and that students should be informed as to the relationship between the goals and the methodology being used to attain those goals.

In The University of Michigan's Pronunciation Laboratory Program (Morley, 1979) students are made aware of how to monitor speech production by manageable bits of information about speech production and with specific techniques (visual, auditory, tactile, and moto-kinesthetic). As Morley explains, the emphasis is placed on the positive as well as the negative aspects of speech behavior, asking the students to observe and describe the positive first and the negative second. Instruction is oriented to the individual learner through more personalized class work. In addition, Morley continues, the standards of satisfactory performance are personalized; intelligibility is the minimum goal, and beyond that it is up to the students to continue to perfect their spoken English to the point which they need in order to function to their own satisfaction.

Teacher Preparation

While teachers might take issue with the natural approach for its failure to suggest any specific activities for pronunciation, teachers cannot ignore its mandate. According to Krashen and Terrell (1983), a central task of the instructor is to present a balance of acquisition and learning activities, which are personalized relative to the goals, age, and abilities of the learner.

In order to utilize any set of pedagogical priorities, teacher preparation is central. As Morley (1975) asserts "the key to the development of a successful program of student self-monitoring is a well-trained teacher who can administer a constructive speech awareness program" (p.85). The undertrained, insecure teacher will overwhelm the learner with superfluous detail; the knowledgeable, confident teacher will select the specific cue to help, not hinder.

For Parish (1977) this means that the teacher should be familiar with articulatory phonetics, English phonology, contrastive analysis, techniques for presenting and modifying pronunciation, and a full range of exercises and drills. To this, Morley (1975) adds:

> Careful training in the dynamics of speech production and the fundamentals of articulatory phonetics—specifically related to English phonology—are necessary. Emphasis must be on speech as a moving process not as a series of static placements or positions (which serve only as convenient "base" descriptions for individual elements). To be able to abstract from this most complex neuro-muscular foundation, the most significant auditory and visual features which will aid the students, a teacher trainee needs thorough knowledge. (p. 85)

Within Strevens' (1984) integrated model of the language learning/teaching process, the informed teacher must be aware of what the learner needs to know and for what purposes, to ensure that the learner will be presented the necessary material, in the appropriate form and time span. Furthermore, Strevens continues, the teacher must be continually aware of the learner's progress to provide learning experiences from which the learner can best profit at a given time. He concludes that informed teaching "entails not only supplying the input of language and other experiences—which in turn means, at least at some stage selecting it—but also deliberately making decisions about quantity, rate, source, content, . . ." (p. 3).

Put simply, pedagogical priorities in the ESL pronunciation class are a question of when to teach what. However, given the above criteria for teacher preparation, decisions regarding the establishment of such priorities based on an assessment of student needs can only be undertaken by well-trained teachers.

In addition to matters of appropriate techniques, approaches, materials, and methodologies, the question of when to teach what is directly addressed in the teacher's organization of the overall learning experience. Strevens (1984) stresses the fact that:

> Learning can be assisted by the organization of the learning experience, by deliberately eliciting input so that the learner progresses in terms of new material, fresh encounters of partly-learned material and re-presentations of material already learned, but also in terms of maintaining impact and so sustaining the learner's volition to learn. Much of the art of teaching lies in successfully carrying out the organization of the learning experience, so that comprehension and learning occur more readily, more rapidly, more effectively, than it would do simply as a result of chance, or as a consequence of "picking up" a language through random encounters with it. (p. 12)

Final Notes

Establishing priorities for the pronunciation class should be not only the teacher's concern, but also the student's. Attention must be focused on the student's role in the learning process. In this regard Stevick (1978) is correct in asserting that the heavy emphasis on work done by the teacher often overshadows the more important, largely internal work of the student. Stevick feels that personality theory and sound group dynamics may prove more important than linguistic analysis and the vowel chart in teaching pronunciation. Fortunately, as Morley points out (1975), more and more teachers are emphasizing the student's involvement in the learning process and the student's responsibility for performance.

Promoting a firm set of pedagogical priorities for the pronunciation class is premature. However, flexible priorities must be based on the assessment of student needs and goals. Priorities beyond the general ones of intelligibility and speech awareness will result only from continued research in interlanguage phonology and the continued development of effective approaches to teaching and learning second language pronunciation.

References

Abraham, R. C. (1984). Patterns in the use of the present tense third person singular -s by university-level ESL speakers. *TESOL Quarterly, 18*(1), 55-69.

Acton, W. (1984). Changing fossilized pronunciation.*TESOL Quarterly, 18*(1), 69-83.

Bialystok, E. (1978). A theoretical model of second language learning. *Language Learning, 28*(1), 69-83.

Fries, C. C. (1945). *Teaching and learning English as a foreign language.* Ann Arbor: The University of Michigan.

Guiora, A., Beit-Hallami, B., Brannon, R. C. L., Dull, C. Y., & Scovel, T. (1972). The effects of experimentally induced changes in ego states on pronunciation ability in a second language: An exploratory study. *Comprehensive Psychiatry, 13,* 421-428.

Heyde, A. (1979). *The relationship between self-esteem and the oral production of a second language.* Unpublished doctoral dissertation, The University of Michigan, Ann Arbor.

Hill, J. H. (1970). Foreign accents, language acquisition, and cerebral dominance revisited. *Language Learning, 20*(2), 237-248.

Krashen, S. (1977). Some issues relating to the monitor model. In H. D. Brown, C. Yorio, & R. Crymes (Eds.), *On TESOL '77* (pp. 144-158). Washington, D.C.: Teachers of English to Speakers of Other Languages.

Krashen, S. (1981). *Second language acquisition and second language learning.* Oxford: Pergamon.

Krashen, S., & Terrell, T. (1983). *The natural approach-Language acquisition in the classroom.* Oxford: Pergamon.

Lenneberg, E. (1967). *The biological foundations of language.* New York: J. Wiley & Sons.

Morley, J. (1975) Round robin on the teaching of pronunciation (in The Forum). *TESOL Quarterly,* 9(1), 83-86.

Morley, J. (1979). *Improving spoken English.* Ann Arbor: The University of Michigan.

Morley, J. (1985). *Principles, activities and techniques for teaching pronunciation.* Unpublished manuscript.

Morley, J. (in press). *Advanced spoken English.* Ann Arbor: The University of Michigan.

Neufeld, G. (1977). Language learning ability in adults: a study on the acquisition of prosodic and articulatory features. *Working Papers in Bilingualism, 12,* 45-60.

Neufeld, G. (1979). Towards a theory of language learning ability. *Language Learning, 29*(2), 227-241.

Neufeld, G. (1980). On the adult's ability to acquire phonology. *TESOL Quarterly, 14*(3), 285-298.

Parish, C. (1977). A practical philosophy of pronunciation. *TESOL Quarterly, 11*(3), 311-317.

Prator, C. (1971). Phonetics vs. phonemics in the ESL classroom: When is allophonic accuracy important? *TESOL Quarterly, 5*(1), 61-72.

Purcell, E. T., & Suter, W. (1980). Predictors of pronunciation accuracy: a re-examination. *Language Learning, 30*(2), 271-287.

Rosansky, E. (1975). *The critical period for the acquisition of language: Some cognitive development considerations.* Unpublished doctoral disertation, Harvard University, Boston.

Scovel, T. (1969). Foreign accents, language acquisition, and cerebral dominance. *Language Learning, 19* (3 & 4), 245-253.

Shen, Y. (1959). Some allophones can be important. *Language Learning, 9*(1 & 2), 7-18.

Stern, H. H. (1975). What can we learn from the good language learner? *Canadian Modern Language Review, 31*(4), 304-318.

Stevick, E. (1978). Toward a practical philosophy of pronunciation: Another view. *TESOL Quarterly, 12*(2), 145-150.

Stockwell, R. P., & Bowen, J. (1965). *The sounds of Spanish and English.* Chicago: The University of Chicago.

Strevens, P. (1984, November) Elements in the language learning/ teaching process: Toward an integrated theory. Paper presented at the meeting of the Japan Association of Language Teachers, Tokyo.

Tarone, E. (1978). The phonology of interlanguage. In J. Richards (Ed.), *Understanding second and foreign language learning* (pp. 15-33). Rowley, MA: Newbury House.

Authors Notes

This paper is dedicated to Professor Naomi Kakita on the occasion of his retirement from Hiroshima University. For over 40 years, Kakita's rigorous application of linguistics and demand for perfection in EFL teacher training has set a standard of excellence throughout Japan that others in the field of English language education will attempt to emulate for years to come. His contribution to the field as a whole is beyond measure.

Footnotes

[1]For a thorough review of IL literature see Tarone (1978); see also Acton (1984).

[2]Scovel's views on cerebral dominance have since moderated, although it is doubtful whether he views native-like L2 pronunciation as a goal attainable by most language learners.

[3]See Bialystok (1978) for a complete discussion of these terms.

Typeset in Alphatype Caledo by
Graftec Corporation, Washington, DC
and lithographed by
Pantograph Printing, Bloomington, IL